PEOPLE YOU SHOULD KNOW

TOP 101 MUSICIANS

Edited by Shalini Saxena

Britannica®
Educational Publishing

IN ASSOCIATION WITH

ROSEN
EDUCATIONAL SERVICES

Published in 2014 by Britannica Educational Publishing (a trademark of Encyclopædia Britannica, Inc.) in association with The Rosen Publishing Group, Inc.
29 East 21st Street, New York, NY 10010

Distributed exclusively by Rosen Publishing.
To see additional Britannica Educational Publishing titles, go to rosenpublishing.com

First Edition

Britannica Educational Publishing
J.E. Luebering: Director, Core Reference Group
Anthony L. Green: Editor, Compton's by Britannica

Rosen Publishing
Hope Lourie Killcoyne: Executive Editor
Shalini Saxena: Editor
Nelson Sá: Art Director
Brian Garvey: Designer
Cindy Reiman: Photography Manager
Marty Levick: Photo Researcher

Library of Congress Cataloging-in-Publication Data

Top 101 musicians/Shalini Saxena, editor. — First edition.
　　pages cm. — (People you should know)
Includes bibliographical references and index.
ISBN 978-1-62275-121-1 (library binding)
1. Musicians—Biography—Dictionaries, Juvenile. 2. Musical groups—Biography—Dictionaries, Juvenile. I. Saxena, Shalini, editor.
ML3929.T66 2014
780.92'2—dc23
[B]

2013033322

Manufactured in the United States of America

On the cover: (Top row, left to right) Madonna *Michael Kappeler/AFP/Getty Images*; Duke Ellington *Michael Ochs Archives/Getty Images*; Ludwig van Beethoven *Georgios Kollidas/Shutterstock.com;* Adele *Jason Merritt/Getty Images*. (Bottom row, left to right) Eminem *Christopher Polk/Getty Images*; Elvis Presley *Archive Photos/Getty Images*; Billie Holiday *Paul Hoeffler/Redferns/Getty Images*; Bob Dylan *Fred Tanneau/AFP/Getty Images*.

Cover and interior pages (top) © iStockphoto.com/René Mansi

CONTENTS

Introduction   vi

Adele   1
Louis Armstrong   3
Johann Sebastian Bach   4
Béla Bartók   6
Count Basie   7
The Beach Boys   9
The Beatles   11
The Bee Gees   14
Ludwig van Beethoven   15
Leonard Bernstein   18
Chuck Berry   19
Black Sabbath   20
David Bowie   20
Johannes Brahms   23
James Brown   24
John Cage   26
Maria Callas   27
Ray Charles   28
Clifton Chenier   30
Frédéric Chopin   31
Eric Clapton   33
The Clash   35
Patsy Cline   37
Nat King Cole   38
Miles Davis   39
Claude Debussy   40
Plácido Domingo   41
Bob Dylan   44
Duke Ellington   47
Eminem   48
Ella Fitzgerald   50
Aretha Franklin   51

1

32

57

61

76

103

George and Ira Gershwin	53
Gilbert and Sullivan	55
Philip Glass	56
Benny Goodman	57
Guido d'Arezzo	59
Woody Guthrie	61
George Frideric Handel	62
W.C. Handy	63
Joseph Haydn	64
Fletcher Henderson	65
Jimi Hendrix	67
Billie Holiday	69
Buddy Holly	70
Charles Ives	71
Mahalia Jackson	73
Michael Jackson	75
Jay-Z	77
Robert Johnson	79
Josquin des Prez	80
B.B. King	81
Umm Kulthūm	82
Leadbelly	84
Led Zeppelin	85
Franz Liszt	86
Little Richard	88
Madonna	89
Gustav Mahler	91
Bob Marley	92
Felix Mendelssohn	95
Joni Mitchell	96
Bill Monroe	97
Wolfgang Amadeus Mozart	99
Muddy Waters	101
Nirvana	103
Charlie Parker	104
Parliament-Funkadelic	106
Luciano Pavarotti	107

Edith Piaf 108
Cole Porter 109
Elvis Presley 110
Prince 112
Public Enemy 112
Giacomo Puccini 114
Tito Puente 115
Radiohead 116
Jimmie Rodgers 119
The Rolling Stones 120
Arnold Schoenberg 122
Franz Schubert 123
Pete Seeger 124
The Sex Pistols 126
Ravi Shankar 128
Dmitri Shostakovich 130
Simon and Garfunkel 130
Frank Sinatra 132
Bessie Smith 135
Smokey Robinson and the Miracles 136
Bruce Springsteen 137
Igor Stravinsky 139
Peter Ilich Tchaikovsky 141
U2 142
Giuseppe Verdi 144
Antonio Vivaldi 145
Richard Wagner 146
Kanye West 148
White Stripes 149
The Who 151
Hank Williams 153
Stevie Wonder 154

Glossary 157
For More Information 159
For Further Reading 162
Index 163

111

129

155

INTRODUCTION

Throughout mankind's history, music has been sung and played in countless ways. From preliterate peoples to more civilized societies, music has always been one of the most defining features of a culture. Through the centuries, musicians have been among the greatest influencers of art, culture, and aesthetics, and the music they have created has often been a mirror of the times in which they lived. Although the 101 musicians profiled in this volume represent a variety of backgrounds, styles, genres, and eras, all have overcome personal and professional challenges to produce some of the world's most enduring and influential pieces.

For each era there are musical icons that represent the cultural and social sensibilities of their time. For example, the early development of Western music was intertwined with the growth of the Christian church. Chanting of scriptures and prayers—a tradition inherited from the time of the Israelite temples in Jerusalem—was practiced by early Christians. By the 6th century CE, modal chant had increased so greatly that Pope Gregory I had it collected and organized, and it came to be called Gregorian chant. In the 11th century, Guido d'Arezzo developed innovations in musical notation that advanced the transcription and learning of melodies, including the well-known hexachord. By the Middle Ages, nonreligious, or secular, music was also being composed by wandering poets who sang of chivalry and courtly love.

Still, it was during the Renaissance that instrumental music freed itself from its dependence on vocal models and emerged as an individual style. Although it continued to be composed "apt for voices or viols," as the Elizabethans put it, music developed that reflected the capabilities of performers and the technical possibilities of instruments. The Baroque period that followed brought forth some of today's most recognizable names in music history. One case is that of Johann Sebastian Bach, who mastered various inventive techniques that revolutionized music, including the fugue—where voices or instrumental parts entered at different points of the composition, each imitating the first before becoming varied and complex—as well as the chorale-prelude.

In contrast to the Baroque period stood the 18th century's ushering in of the Classical Age, in which composers such as Haydn, Mozart, and Beethoven resisted the complexity of Baroque-period works and developed compositions that were dignified, emotionally restrained, and marked by great clarity. Classical music progressed until Ludwig van Beethoven brought it to a new period, initiating the then-shocking practice of dissonance, or clashing chords.

The Romantic period saw a further shedding of the confines of set forms. Romantic composers enjoyed writing music that was more pictorial than earlier works and often attempted to imitate nature. The German composer Johannes Brahms stands out as a key figure from this period and was considered an heir to Bach and Beethoven's prior successes. In the 19th century, the Romantic period led to the development of the great operas of Italy and France.

By the turn of the 20th century musical works were becoming more widely known through technological advances. Composers were searching for new kinds of musical expression. Their new styles were a reaction against the emotional excesses of the Romantic school. It was at this time that the jazz, blues, and swing movements grew in popularity in the United States. Jazz musicians Louis Armstrong, Duke Ellington, and the rich-voiced Bessie Smith are among the iconic figures of the 1920s. Singers such as Ella Fitzgerald—a popular favorite among swing scat vocalists—and Billie Holiday—who was only a teenager when she began her singing career—helped the style to grow into a widespread phenomenon.

The blues and jazz genres gave way to 1950s' rock 'n' roll artists. Elvis Presley is a quintessential example. The music he created in the 1950s and '60s showcased a unique blend of influences across color lines and was marked by a compelling mix of energy and provocative style of delivery. Produced during a period of social upheaval—which included the early days of the civil rights movement—his music spoke to a generation more socially progressive than any that came before, making him enormously popular.

In the 1960s several influences combined to lift rock out of the bland and mechanical format into which it had already declined. In England, where rock's development had been slow, the Beatles and the Rolling Stones were found to have retained the freshness of its very early years, and they achieved enormous success in the United States. At the same time, artists such as Bob Dylan and Joni Mitchell were blending the traditional ballads and verse forms of folk music with rock, and musicians began to explore social and political themes. Rock and soul music—especially the sophisticated but hook-laden variety of the latter, represented in the music of such artists as Aretha Franklin—quickly attracted the allegiance of Western teenagers.

Through the 1970s and '80s, the world of music entered new dimensions with the advent of electronic media and changes in recording styles. Rock music paved a path for new genres, including folk, disco, punk rock, and heavy metal. The arrival of MTV in 1981 led to the proliferation of music videos, a new visual form to represent popular songs championed in its early days by artists such as Michael Jackson and Madonna. The 1990s saw the rise of alternative rock, hip-hop, and rap as popular styles. By the late 1990s hip-hop had become the best-selling genre of popular music in the United States and also a global phenomenon. Today, digital audio formats and file sharing on the Internet have helped all forms of music reach new parts of the globe in ways unimaginable in the period when Arezzo was developing notation.

In these pages, readers are invited to peek into the times, triumphs, and tragedies of the musical geniuses of various eras. It is an essential guide for any music lover who wants to know more about the musicians who have given us all so much listening joy.

ADELE

(b. 1988–)

A dele Laurie Blue Adkins was born on May 5, 1988, in Tottenham, London, England. She was raised by a young single mother in various working-class neighborhoods of London. As a child, she enjoyed singing contemporary pop music and learned to play the guitar and the clarinet. However, it was not until her early teens, when she discovered rhythm-and-blues singer Etta James and other mid-20th century performers that she began to consider a musical career. While she honed her talents at a government-funded secondary school for the performing arts, a friend began posting songs Adkins had written and recorded onto the social networking website Myspace. Her music eventually caught the attention of record labels, and in 2006, several months after graduating she signed a contract with XL Recordings.

After building anticipation in Britain with some well-received live performances, Adele (as she now billed herself) released her first album, *19*, in 2008. (The title referred to the age at which she penned most of the tracks.) The recording debuted at number one on

Adele holding the Academy Award for Best Original Song at the Dolby Theatre, Hollywood, Calif. *s_bukleys/Shutterstock*

the British album chart, and critics praised Adele's supple phrasing, tasteful arrangements, and ability to channel her intimate emotional experiences (especially with heartbreak) into songs that had wide resonance. She also earned comparisons to Amy Winehouse, another young British singer conspicuously influenced by soul music. A performance on the television program *Saturday Night Live* helped introduce Adele to American audiences, and in early 2009, she won the Grammy Awards for Best New Artist and Best Female Pop Vocal Performance (for the lush bluesy song "Chasing Pavements").

For her next album, Adele enlisted a number of songwriters and producers, including Rick Rubin, to collaborate with her. The result, *21* (2011), was a bolder and more stylistically diverse set of material, with singles ranging from the earthy-gospel and disco-inflected "Rolling in the Deep" to the affecting breakup ballad "Someone like You." Both songs hit number one in several countries, and, despite a vocal-cord ailment that forced Adele to cancel numerous tour dates in 2011, the album became the biggest-selling release of the year in both the United States and the United Kingdom.

After undergoing throat surgery in November 2011, Adele faced questions about her future as a performing artist. However, she staged a powerhouse performance at the 2012 Grammy Awards ceremony in February where she collected six Grammy trophies, including best album for *21*. She also won two awards (for best record and song of the year) for the "Rolling in the Deep." Days later, she received two Brit Awards (the British equivalent of the Grammys) for best album and best female solo artist. The subsequent sales spike for her *21* album further confirmed the singer's emergence as a commercial success. Her soulful, emotive voice and traditionally crafted songs made her one of the most broadly popular performers of her generation.

Additionally, with worldwide sales of more than 17 million copies by January 2012, *21* was credited with helping revive the flagging recording industry. Adele remained in the spotlight with the release of the blockbuster James Bond movie *Skyfall* (2012), for which she provided the Academy Award–winning theme song. In 2013 she won the Grammy for Best Pop Solo Performance for "Set Fire to the Rain" from the concert album *Live at the Royal Albert Hall* (2011).

LOUIS ARMSTRONG

(b. 1901–d. 1971)

Louis Daniel Armstrong—popularly known as Satchmo and Pops—was born on Aug. 4, 1901, in New Orleans, the birthplace of American jazz. His father, Willie, was a day laborer in a turpentine plant, and his mother, Mayann (Mary Ann), worked chiefly as a domestic help. His grandparents had been slaves. Dippermouth (his original nickname) picked up small change by singing and dancing with other street children in the notorious Storyville district.

After Armstrong celebrated New Year's Eve by firing a .38 pistol that belonged to one of his "stepfathers," he was sent to the Colored Waifs' Home for Boys in 1913. There he tried several instruments until he found his voice in the cornet, and, though self-taught, he became the leader of the school band. He learned to blow on a bugle in reform school when he was 13.

Armstrong was 18 when he replaced his idol, King Oliver, in Kid Ory's Brownskin Band. A mellophonist taught him how to read music when he joined a Mississippi riverboat band. In 1922 he went to Chicago to play second cornet with Oliver's Creole Jazz Band. His time with Fletcher Henderson's big band in New York City in 1924 expanded his music beyond the traditional New Orleans style. Soon he switched to the trumpet on theater dates because of its brighter sound and flashier look. His genius for improvisation changed the course of jazz, but after the 1940s he had his greatest success as a pop singer.

The first band built in the image of one personality was the one Armstrong organized in Chicago in 1925. With his phenomenal tone, instrumental range, stamina, and stunning gift for melodic variations, he was able to turn jazz from ensemble music to a solo art. His Hot Five and Hot Seven recordings were jazz landmarks. He introduced scat on "Heebie Jeebies," supposedly because he dropped the sheet music. The voice was first used as an instrument on "Skid-Dat-De-Dat," also the first tune built completely on breaks. "With Cornet Chop Suey" he had created the stop-time solo break. Another Armstrong innovation was high-register playing in jazz, and his sandpaper voice influenced more conventional jazz singing.

Armstrong's contagious cheer and flamboyant style made him an ideal goodwill ambassador for American music. In 1933, during his first European tour, he dedicated a hot trumpet break to King George VI with "This one's for you, Rex!" As his non-jazz audience grew, he appeared frequently on television and made more than 35 film shorts or movies, including *High Society* and *Hello, Dolly!*

Satchmo classics include "West End Blues," "Weather Bird," "Tight Like This," "Hotter than That," and "S.O.L. Blues." Among his best-selling records were "Mack the Knife" and "C'est si bon."

The musician had four wives—Daisy Parker, a prostitute (1918); Lil (Lillian) Hardin, a jazz pianist who gave him some formal musical education (1924); Alpha Smith (1938); and Lucille Wilson, a showgirl (1942). He died on July 6, 1971, in New York City.

JOHANN SEBASTIAN BACH

(b. 1685–d. 1750)

Johann Sebastian Bach was born on March 21, 1685, in Eisenach, Thuringia (now Germany). Orphaned when he was 10, Bach was cared for by his eldest brother. In 1700 he became part of a select choir of poor boys at the school of Michaeliskirche, Lüneburg. By the time he left two years later, he was a skilled organist and composer. His first major positions, as the official organist for a duke at Weimar and as the organist at the Neue Kirche (New Church) in Arnstadt, both began in 1703, while he was still a teenager. His duties included composing sacred cantatas, a type of music for use during church services.

In 1707 Bach left Arnstadt and obtained a position at Mühlhausen. There he produced several more church cantatas, all cast in a conservative mold, based on biblical and chorale texts; these did not display the influence of the "modern" Italian operatic forms that were to appear in his later cantatas. His famous organ "Toccata and Fugue in D Minor," written in the rhapsodic northern style, and the "Prelude and Fugue in D Major" were probably composed during this period. In 1708

Bach resigned from his work at Mühlhausen and took a post at Weimar, Thuringia.

At Weimar, Bach was court organist and a member of the orchestra. These are the years that his style underwent a profound change. He was influenced by the new styles and forms of the contemporary Italian opera and by the innovations of such Italian concerto composers as Antonio Vivaldi. Among other works almost certainly composed at Weimar are most of the *Orgelbüchlein* (*Little Organ Book*), all but the last of the so-called 18 "Great" chorale preludes, the earliest organ trios, and most of the organ preludes and fugues. Through his years at Weimar, Bach steadily attained more demanding positions, in 1714 becoming concertmaster, with the duty of composing a cantata every month. Two years later, however, when the music director at Weimar died, Bach was overlooked for the position, leading to his departure from Weimar the next year.

From 1717 to 1723 Bach served as music director at Köthen. During this time he was concerned chiefly with chamber and orchestral music. Even though some of the works may have been composed earlier and revised later, it was at Köthen that many of his sonatas were put into something like their present form. He finished the *Brandenburg Concertos*, as well as the first book (1722) of *The Well-Tempered Clavier*, which would eventually consist of two books, each of 24 preludes and fugues in all keys and known as "the Forty-Eight."

In 1723 Bach became the director of church music for the city of Leipzig and was in charge of the music at four churches. During his first two or three years, he produced a large number of new cantatas, sometimes at the rate of one a week. As a result of creating this overabundance of church music, which would meet his future needs at services for some time, after 1726 Bach turned his attention to other projects. For many years he was honorary music director at Weissenfels as well as director of the Leipzig Collegium Musicum ("Musical Society"). For the concerts he produced during this time, he adapted some of his earlier concerti as harpsichord concerti, thus becoming one of the first composers—if not the very first—of concerti for keyboard instrument and orchestra.

Bach created hundreds of musical compositions, including works for choir, orchestra, and individual instruments, especially the organ. His works brought to a climax the Baroque period, during which many new forms and styles were developed. Combining elements of the Lutheran chorale, the French and Italian orchestral styles, and Baroque organ music, Bach produced the *Brandenburg Concertos* (1721) for orchestra, *The Well-Tempered Clavier* (1722–44) for keyboard, the *St. John* (1723) and *St. Matthew* (1729) passions, nearly 200 cantatas, and the *Mass in B Minor* (completed about 1738).

Married twice, Bach fathered 20 children, 10 of whom survived to adulthood. Several of his sons also became successful composers, including Wilhelm Friedemann Bach, Carl Philipp Emanuel Bach, and Johann Christian Bach. After a productive career, Johann Sebastian died in Leipzig on July 28, 1750.

Although his music was ignored as old-fashioned for quite a few years after his death, it underwent a revival in the early 1800s. His work had a profound influence on musical geniuses such as Joseph Haydn, Wolfgang Amadeus Mozart, and Ludwig van Beethoven as well as upon many musicians since that time, and Bach's music remained popular into the 21st century.

BÉLA BARTÓK

(b. 1881–d. 1945)

Hungarian composer-pianist Béla Bartók was a major force in the 20th-century musical world. He was born in Nagyszentmiklós, Hungary (now Sînnicolau Mare, Romania), on March 25, 1881. His father, director of an agricultural college, was a talented amateur musician. His mother gave Béla his first piano lessons when he was five. After his father's death in 1888, his mother went to work as a piano teacher. Eventually she settled in Pozsony (now Bratislava, Slovakia).

In 1899 Bartók entered the Royal Academy of Music in Budapest, devoting himself to the study of the piano. The music of Richard Strauss inspired his first major composition, "Kossuth" (1903), a symphonic poem. Bartók was appointed professor of piano at the Royal Academy in 1907, a position he held for the next 30 years. In 1909 he married Marta Ziegler, one of his pupils. After their divorce, in 1923, Bartók married Ditta Pásztory, another pupil.

An interest in the folk songs of the Hungarian peasants led Bartók to travel the countryside, collecting and recording melodies. Their influence soon became evident in many of his own compositions—"Duke Bluebeard's Castle" (1911); "The Miraculous Mandarin" (1919); and the "Dance Suite" of 1923.

Although his works were not popular in Hungary, Bartók's reputation was growing abroad. During the 1920s and 1930s he performed his own piano compositions on tour in Europe and the United States. Some of his

Béla Bartók. *Popperfoto/Getty Images*

best-known works include *Cantata Profana* (1930), his fifth and sixth string quartets (1934, 1939), and a sonata for two pianos and percussion (1937).

In 1940, because of the growing Nazi influence in Hungary, the Bartóks left for the United States, where the composer's health began to fail and he suffered severe financial difficulties. The popular *Concerto for Orchestra* (1943) was one of his last completed works. On Sept. 26, 1945, Bartók died of leukemia in a New York City hospital.

COUNT BASIE

(b. 1904–d. 1984)

U.S. jazz pianist, composer, and bandleader Count Basie was one of the outstanding organizers of big bands in jazz history. He transformed big-band jazz by the simplicity of his arrangements and secured his place in history with such classic numbers as "One O'Clock Jump" and "Basie Boogie."

William Basie was born on Aug. 21, 1904, in Red Bank, N.J. He studied music with his mother and was later influenced by the Harlem pianists James P. Johnson and Fats Waller, receiving informal training on the organ from Waller. He began his professional career as an accompanist on the vaudeville circuit. Basie eventually settled in Kansas City, Mo., and in 1935 assumed the leadership of a nine-piece band, composed of former members of the Walter Page and Bennie Moten orchestras.

One night, while the band was broadcasting on a short-wave radio station in Kansas City, the announcer dubbed him "Count" Basie to compete with such other bandleaders as Duke Ellington. The jazz critic John Hammond heard the broadcasts in New York City and promptly launched the band on its career in Chicago. Although rooted in the riff style of the 1930s swing-era bands, the Basie band included soloists who reflected the styles of their own periods. In this way the band was a springboard for such artists as tenor saxophonist Lester Young, trumpeter Buck Clayton, and trumpeter-composer Thad Jones. Many musicians considered Basie's to be the major big band in jazz history, a model for ensemble rhythmic conception and tonal balance.

During the late 1930s the accompanying unit for the band (pianist Basie, rhythm guitarist Freddie Green, bassist Walter Page, and drummer Jo Jones) was unique in its lightness, precision, and relaxation, becoming the precursor for modern jazz accompanying styles. Basie's syncopated and spare but exquisitely timed chording, commonly termed comping, became the model for what was expected from combo pianists in their improvised accompaniments for the next 30 years of jazz. Despite its influence on modern piano styles, Basie's solo technique had roots in the pre-swing-era style of Fats Waller, and Basie continued to display such a "stride style" in performances through the 1970s.

Basie's autobiography, *Good Morning Blues*, written with Albert Murray, was published in 1985, one year after his death. Count Basie died on Apr. 26, 1984, in Hollywood, Fla., leaving a grand legacy of song that would continue to influence jazz musicians for generations to come.

THE BEACH BOYS

The U.S. rock group the Beach Boys blended pleasing melodies and distinctive vocals to portray a youthful, laid-back southern California lifestyle of the 1960s. The original members were Brian Wilson (b. June 20, 1942, Inglewood, Calif.), Dennis Wilson (b. Dec. 4, 1944, Inglewood–d. Dec. 28, 1983, Marina del Rey, Calif.), Carl Wilson (b. Dec. 21, 1946, Los Angeles, Calif.–d. Feb. 6, 1998, Los Angeles), Michael Love (b. March 15, 1941, Los Angeles), and Alan Jardine (b. Sept. 3, 1942, Lima, Ohio). Significant later members included David Marks (b. Aug. 22, 1948, Newcastle, Penn.) and Bruce Johnston (b. Benjamin Baldwin; June 27, 1942, Chicago, Ill.).

Growing up in suburban Los Angeles, the Wilson brothers were encouraged by their parents to explore music. Their father, who operated a small machinery shop, was also a songwriter. While still teenagers, Brian, drummer Dennis, and guitarist Carl joined with cousin Love and friends Jardine and Marks to write and perform pop music in the spirit of Chuck Berry, who greatly influenced the group.

Dennis, a novice surfer, talked Brian and the rest of the group (then called the Pendletons) into writing songs about the emerging sport. With the success in 1961 of their first single, "Surfin'," the Beach Boys signed with Capitol Records. Brian's ambitions as a pop composer took flight, and for years he would write almost all the group's songs, often with collaborators (most frequently Love). The Beach Boys' songs about cars and surfing, including "409" and "Surfin' Safari," helped their debut album reach number 14. Their follow-up single "Surfin' U.S.A." and its album of the same name were commercial successes in 1963, and Brian assumed complete artistic control. With their next album, *Surfer Girl*, he was writer, arranger, and producer. He was gifted at creating songs with crisp rock roots (for example, "Little Deuce Coupe," "Fun, Fun, Fun," and "I Get Around").

After the first of a series of stress- and drug-related breakdowns in 1964, Brian withdrew from touring. He was replaced first by

9

singer-guitarist Glen Campbell, then by veteran surf singer-musician Bruce Johnston. Brian focused thereafter on the Beach Boys' studio work, and the album *Pet Sounds* appeared in 1966, with "Good Vibrations"—which reached number one in the autumn of 1966—following. When the album *Smile* failed to be ready by its due date in December, however, Brian went into seclusion; the rest of the band hurried to compile and release a version of that work titled *Smiley Smile* (1967).

For the remainder of the decade, the Beach Boys released records that were increasingly inconsistent both commercially and musically. In 1970 the band signed with Warner Brothers. After the album *Sunflower* sold poorly, Brian became a recluse, experimenting with hallucinogens while the rest of the group produced several modest-selling albums. *Endless Summer*, a greatest hits compilation, reached number one in the charts in 1974.

In 1976, Brian, still addicted to drugs, emerged with the commercially successful album *15 Big Ones*. The next year Dennis released a critically acclaimed solo album, *Pacific Ocean Blue*. In 1988 Brian released a self-titled solo album, the other Beach Boys had a number one hit with "Kokomo," and the group was inducted into the Rock and Roll Hall of Fame. In the 1990s the Beach Boys continued to tour and record. Brian released another solo album and collaborated on an album with his daughters Carnie and Wendy, who were successful performers in their own right. In 1998 the Beach Boys released *Endless Harmony*, a collection based on an acclaimed television documentary on the group.

In 2004, Brian released "Getting' in over My Head," with contributions from Paul McCartney, Eric Clapton, and Elton John. That same year he presented *Smile*, which he had spent nearly four decades fine-tuning. After being presented with a Kennedy Center Honor in 2007, Brian released *That Lucky Old Sun* (2008), a nostalgic celebration of southern California. In 2012 the main surviving members reunited for a celebratory tour. The concerts coincided with the release of *That's Why God Made the Radio*, the group's first album in two decades to feature original material.

THE BEATLES

A quartet of talented musicians from Liverpool, England, the Beatles generated a phenomenal run of gold records that endured long after the rock group disbanded. Affectionately nicknamed the Fab Four, the band started a worldwide frenzy of fandom in the 1960s called Beatlemania. Their music, rooted in American rock and roll but liberally flavored with rhythm and blues and rockabilly, featured harmonic vocals, melodic guitar, and a driving backbeat that influenced scores of young musicians and revolutionized popular music. As musicians, as composers, and as entertainers, the Beatles bridged generation gaps and language barriers, reshaping rock music with their wit and sophistication. As trendsetters of youth counterculture, they popularized long hair, mod dress, hallucinogenic drugs, Indian music, and Eastern mysticism.

The three guitarists in the group—John Lennon (b. Oct. 9, 1940–d. Dec. 8, 1980), Paul McCartney (b. June 18, 1942), and George Harrison (b. Feb. 25, 1943–d. Nov. 29, 2001)—first played together as schoolboys in the late 1950s with a band named the Quarrymen. The group was renamed Johnny and the Moondogs, the Moonshiners, then the Silver Beatles (a wordplay on the musical term "beat" that also paid tribute to rocker Buddy Holly's Crickets). Drummer Pete Best (b. Nov. 24, 1941) joined the band in 1960, and Stu Sutcliffe (b. June 23, 1940–d. Apr. 10, 1962) played bass for them for several months that year. After Sutcliffe left the band, McCartney switched to playing bass.

The band performed regularly in Liverpool as well as Hamburg, Germany. In Liverpool, they became a regular fixture at the Cavern Club, where they caught the attention of local record-shop owner Brian Epstein, who offered to manage the band. Epstein had the group shed its stage-wear of leather jackets for more respectable suit jackets and ties. In 1962 the band—now known as simply the Beatles—fired Best and replaced him with another Liverpool drummer, Ringo Starr (byname of Richard Starkey; b. July 7, 1940). Epstein secured a recording contract

Fans of the Beatles, including two girls wearing sweatshirts with images of its four members, await the band's arrival in New York City in 1964. The fervor over the Beatles was representative of Beatlemania. *Keystone/Hulton Archive/Getty Images*

for the band and convinced record producer George Martin to produce the first songs of the Lennon and McCartney songwriting team.

Most of the Beatles' early recordings feature fairly straightforward pop love songs. Their first record—a Lennon-McCartney song called "Love Me Do"—was released in October 1962 and became an immediate hit. By the time they led the so-called British invasion of the United States in 1964, the band held the top five spots on the singles recording charts and had released their first film, *A Hard Day's Night*. Within a year, six of their albums in succession hit the top of the charts, and *Help!*, an antic musical film, opened to critical acclaim. By then Beatlemania was a global phenomenon.

But there were also controversial incidents, such as the group's rebuff of an invitation to a meeting with leaders of the Philippines and Lennon's remark to a reporter that the Beatles were more popular than Jesus Christ. While Lennon apologized for his statement, he continued to cause controversy in the years to come. By 1966, the strain of constant touring coupled with the pressure of being the world's most popular musicians had taken its toll, and the band announced their retirement from live performances, stating that they would focus on studio work.

In 1967 the Beatles released *Sgt. Pepper's Lonely Hearts Club Band*. The album demonstrated the group's dramatic evolution in music and personal appearance. The Beatles' songs featured complex orchestration and cryptic lyrics, while their formerly clean-shaven faces sported moustaches.

The later Beatles albums were like variety shows—a miscellany of rock, blues, country, folk, ballads, social commentary, nursery rhymes, 1920s parodies, and satires of other pop groups, with an occasional injection of surrealism. Most of their material was credited to Lennon and McCartney as a team; in time Lennon's sardonic songs were recognizable because they were generally composed in the first person, while McCartney's songs developed scenarios with offbeat characters. In addition to the landmark *Sgt. Pepper's* album, their most acclaimed works were the innovative *Revolver* (1966); the exuberant *The Beatles* (1968), commonly referred to as the "White Album"; and their last joint effort, *Abbey Road* (1969). (*Let It Be*, issued in 1970, had been delayed for simultaneous release with a film and book.)

The Beatles officially broke up in 1970. Lennon had begun recording with his second wife, the avant-garde conceptual artist Yoko Ono, and McCartney formed the successful soft-rock group Wings with his wife, Linda. Harrison and Starr also recorded solo albums.

Rumors that the Beatles would reunite persisted for a decade after the band's demise until Lennon was murdered in New York City in 1980. In 1995 an anthology of the band's recordings was released alongside a video catalog of their history together. Harrison, McCartney, and Starr reunited to issue two new recordings for the project from previously unrecorded material. Using state-of-the-art recording technology, the voice of John Lennon was incorporated into the tracks. Although the public camaraderie of the three surviving Beatles following the project ignited hopes for a reunion tour, the musicians made clear their decision to leave the past in the past. With Harrison's death in 2001 after a battle with cancer, the hope of a reunion tour was finally laid to rest.

THE BEE GEES

Beginning in the late 1950s Australian pop music group the Bee Gees (brothers Barry, Maurice, and Robin Gibb) parlayed their high harmonies and catchy pop tunes to become one of the most successful groups in pop music history. With their multiplatinum albums and hit singles—including the sound track recording for the feature film *Saturday Night Fever* (1977), which eventually sold more than 30 million copies worldwide—the Bee Gees became international sensations during the disco boom of the 1970s.

Barry was born on Sept. 1, 1946, in Manchester, England, and his twin brothers, Robin and Maurice, were born on Dec. 22, 1949, on the Isle of Man. (Maurice Gibb died in Miami, Florida, on Jan. 12, 2003, and Robin Gibb died in London, England, on May 20, 2012.) Their father, Hugh, was a bandleader, and the brothers began performing at a young age. After the family moved from England to Brisbane, Australia, in 1958, the Gibb brothers started performing in talent shows and other amateur outlets where they sang Everly Brothers songs and occasionally one of Barry's compositions. While still teenagers they were signed by Australia's Festival Records in 1962 and released several albums and numerous singles before landing their first hit with "Spicks and Specks" (1967). Relocating to England, the group picked up a drummer and bass player as well as a manager, Robert Stigwood, founder of RSO Records, who had been associated with the Beatles. Under Stigwood's guidance the group produced a number of hits in the United States and Britain: "New York Mining Disaster 1941" (1967); "To Love Somebody" (1967); "Holiday" (1967); "Massachusetts" (1967); "Words" (1968); "I've Got to Get a Message to You" (1968); and "I Started a Joke" (1969).

In the early 1970s the band went through a period of upheaval as nonfamily members left and the brothers fought among themselves. Despite having several hits—"Lonely Days" (1970) and "How Can You Mend a Broken Heart?" (1971)—the group also released a number of flops. Stigwood recruited a new producer for the band and brought them to Miami, where they developed a funk-falsetto sound that produced the hits "Jive Talkin'" (1975), "Nights on Broadway" (1975), "You Should Be Dancing" (1976), and "Love So Right" (1976). Subsequently, Stigwood asked the Bee Gees to contribute tracks to *Saturday Night Fever* (1977), a disco film he was producing. The movie and its sound track, including the Bee Gees' "Stayin' Alive," "Night Fever," and "How Deep Is Your Love?" became smash hits and made them international stars.

Following *Saturday Night Fever* the Bee Gees had three more number one hits with "Too Much Heaven," "Tragedy," and "Love You Inside and Out," from their *Spirits Having Flown* (1979) album. Although the sound track to the film *Stayin' Alive* (1983), the critically panned sequel to *Saturday Night Fever*, went platinum, the brothers took off in different directions in the 1980s as they tried to distance themselves from disco. They spent most of the decade recording as songwriters and soloists as well as serving as producers for other artists. Barry Gibb produced and sang duets with Barbra Streisand on her *Guilty* (1980) album and wrote songs for Dionne Warwick, Diana Ross, and Kenny Rogers. The brothers reunited in 1987 with a new album, *E-S-P* (1987), which topped the charts in Britain and Germany but barely made the charts in the United States.

In the 1990s, the Bee Gees continued recording and occasionally played concerts and charity events. They released several new compilations, and their *Still Waters* (1997) album made the top ten on the British charts. After careers of more than 30 years in rock and roll, the Bee Gees were inducted into the Rock and Roll Hall of Fame in May 1997.

LUDWIG VAN BEETHOVEN

(b. 1770–d. 1827)

Ludwig van Beethoven created a bridge between the 18th-century classical period and the new beginnings of Romanticism. His music expressed the new spirit of humanism as well as the ideals of the French Revolution, with its passionate concern for the freedom and dignity of the individual.

Ludwig van Beethoven was born in Bonn, Germany, and was baptized on Dec. 17, 1770. His father and grandfather worked as court musicians in Bonn. His father, a singer, gave him his early musical training. Although he had only meager academic schooling, he studied piano, violin, and French horn, and before he was 12 years old he became a court organist. His first important teacher of composition was Christian Gottlob Neefe. In 1787 he studied briefly with Wolfgang Amadeus Mozart, and five years later he left Bonn permanently and went to Vienna to study with Joseph Haydn and later with Antonio Salieri.

Beethoven's first public appearance in Vienna was on March 29, 1795, as a soloist in one of his piano concerti. Even before he left Bonn, he had developed a reputation for fine improvisatory performances. In Vienna young Beethoven soon had a long list of aristocratic patrons who loved music and were eager to help him.

ONSET OF DEAFNESS AND ILL HEALTH

In the late 1700s Beethoven began to suffer from early symptoms of deafness and from severe abdominal pain. By 1802 Beethoven was convinced that his deafness not only was permanent but was getting progressively worse. He spent that summer in the country and wrote what has become known as the "Heiligenstadt Testament." In the document, apparently intended for his two brothers, Beethoven expressed his humiliation and despair. For the rest of his life he searched for a cure for his ailments, but his abdominal distress persisted and by 1819 his deafness had become total. Afterward, in order to have conversations with his friends, Beethoven had them write down their questions and replied orally.

Beethoven never married. Although he had many friends, he seemed to be a lonely man, and he was prone to irritability and dramatic mood swings. He continued to appear in public but spent more and more of his time working on his compositions. He lived in various villages near Vienna and took long walks carrying sketchbooks in which he would write down his musical ideas. Scholars who have studied these sketchbooks have discovered the agonizingly long process that the composer went through in order to perfect his melodies, harmonies, and instrumentations.

THREE PERIODS OF WORK

Most critics divide Beethoven's work into three general periods, omitting the earliest years of his apprenticeship in Bonn. Although some pieces do not fit exactly into the scheme, these divisions can be used to categorize the composer's work.

The first period, from 1794 to about 1800, includes music generally typical of the classical

Bust of Ludwig van Beethoven. *Universal Images Group/Getty Images*

era. The influence of such musicians as Mozart and Haydn is evident in Beethoven's early work, though he added his own subtleties, including sudden changes of dynamics.

The second period, from 1801 to 1814, includes works with many techniques derived from improvisation, such as surprising rhythmic accents and other unexpected elements. His works also expanded in length, complexity, and depth of feeling. His *Third Symphony*, known as the *Eroica*, and *Fourth Piano Concerto* are fine examples of this period.

The final period, from 1814 to the end of his life, is characterized by a concentration of musical ideas and even wider ranges of harmony and counterpoint. The last string quartets contain some of the composer's most vivid new ideas. Beethoven created longer and more complicated forms of music, including his titanic *Ninth Symphony*.

Many critics and listeners regard Beethoven as the finest composer who ever lived. His music was unique and emotional. Never before had instrumental music, which had previously been considered inferior to vocal music, been brought to such heights. He also made great strides with chamber music for piano, as well as for string quartets, trios, and sonatas. His works include 9 symphonies, 32 piano sonatas, 5 piano concerti, 17 string quartets, a violin concerto, 10 sonatas for violin and piano, an opera (*Fidelio*), the *Mass in C Major*, and the mass known as *Missa Solemnis*.

Beethoven died in Vienna on March 26, 1827. His funeral was attended by some 20,000 mourners. The bicentennial of his birth and the sesquicentennial of his death were celebrated with new performances and recordings of all of the master's works.

LEONARD BERNSTEIN

(b. 1918–d. 1990)

Leonard Bernstein was born on Aug. 25, 1918, in Lawrence, Mass. He studied composition with Walter Piston at Harvard University. Upon graduating in 1939 he entered the Curtis Institute of Music, in Philadelphia, Pa., to study conducting, orchestration, and piano. Bernstein then went on to perfect his conducting technique with Serge Koussevitzky at the Berkshire Music Center, at Tanglewood, Mass., in the summers of 1940 and 1941.

In 1943 Bernstein was appointed assistant conductor of the New York Philharmonic. His first notable success came on November 14 of that year when he had the opportunity to substitute for an ailing conductor. Bernstein's technical self-assurance under difficult circumstances and his interpretive excellence made an immediate impression and marked the beginning of a brilliant career.

He subsequently conducted the New York City Center orchestra from 1945 to 1947 and appeared as guest conductor in the United States, in Europe, and in Israel. In 1958 he became permanent conductor of the

New York Philharmonic, sometimes appearing as piano soloist while conducting from the keyboard. With this orchestra he made many recordings and several international tours. In 1969 he retired, becoming laureate conductor.

His accomplishments both in serious music and for the Broadway stage and his flair for teaching young people combined to make Leonard Bernstein a well-known conductor, composer, and teacher. The popularity of this American musical genius increased through his appearances on television, not only as conductor and pianist, but also as commentator and entertainer.

A great range of music emerged from Bernstein as a composer, often using jazz rhythms and religious themes. His *Jeremiah Symphony* (first performed in 1944) was the first of a number of works to embody elements of Hebrew music. He wrote Mass for the opening of the John F. Kennedy Center for the Performing Arts, in Washington, D.C., in September 1971. His ballet *Fancy Free* (1944) was expanded into a full-scale musical comedy, *On the Town*, in the same year, the first of a series of shows that included *Wonderful Town* (1953) and *Candide* (1956) and culminated in the popular *West Side Story* (1957). He also published collections of his lectures. Bernstein died on Oct. 14, 1990, in New York City.

CHUCK BERRY

(b. 1926–)

Born on Oct. 18, 1926, in St. Louis, Mo., Chuck Berry was one of the most influential figures of rock 'n' roll music. In 1955 he was recommended to the president of Chess Records by Muddy Waters. Chess released most of Berry's hit singles, including "Maybellene," "Roll Over Beethoven," and "Johnny B. Goode." Berry was also exciting onstage, performing his famous "duck-walk" while playing guitar. His career took a downturn in the 1960s, but his later albums sold well, and Berry was considered a music legend. He was inducted into the Rock and Roll Hall of Fame in 1986.

BLACK SABBATH

B ritish band Black Sabbath produced an aggressive brand of rock music that defined the term "heavy" metal in the 1970s. The principal members were Ozzy Osbourne (John Osbourne; b. Dec. 3, 1948, Birmingham, Warwickshire, England), Terry "Geezer" Butler (b. July 17, 1949, Birmingham), Tony Iommi (b. Feb. 19, 1948, Birmingham), and Bill Ward (b. May 5, 1948, Birmingham).

Osbourne, Butler, Iommi, and Ward were schoolmates in Birmingham, England, in the late 1960s and first formed the blues bands Polka Tulk and Earth. These earlier bands evolved into Black Sabbath. The group's name came from a Butler song that was inspired by a Boris Karloff movie.

Black Sabbath cultivated a dark and foreboding image with ominous guitar riffs, slow-churn tempos, and Osbourne's sullen vocals. The band's lyrics, full of occult imagery, and coarse musicianship were reviled by critics and shunned by radio programmers. Constant touring, however, turned the band members into stars, and songs such as "Paranoid," "Iron Man," and "War Pigs" became metal classics. By the end of the 1970s they had sold millions of records and had become the standard by which virtually every heavy metal band had to measure itself.

Osbourne left the band in the late 1970s, and Ward and Butler later followed him out. Iommi kept the Black Sabbath name alive throughout the 1980s with a variety of musicians. Osbourne remained in the spotlight, forging a solo career marked by outrageous drug-fueled antics and best-selling albums. *The Osbournes* (2002–05), a reality television show on MTV that followed Osbourne and his family, was hugely popular. In the 1990s the original lineup reunited on several occasions. Black Sabbath was inducted into the Rock and Roll Hall of Fame in 2006.

DAVID BOWIE

(b. 1947–)

B ritish singer, songwriter, and actor David Bowie, with his outlandish costumes, chameleon-like personalities, and musical diversity, reigned as the king of glam-rock in the 1970s. He was born David Robert Jones on Jan. 8, 1947, in London to Haywood Stenton Jones and Margaret Mary Burns. David was raised in a poor section of London. He became interested in music at an early age; his parents exposed him to the music of American rockers Elvis Presley and Little Richard, and he took up the guitar and tenor saxophone. In high school he studied commercial art, which prepared him for a short stint as a graphic artist at an advertising agency. Meanwhile, he had formed a succession of rhythm and blues groups,

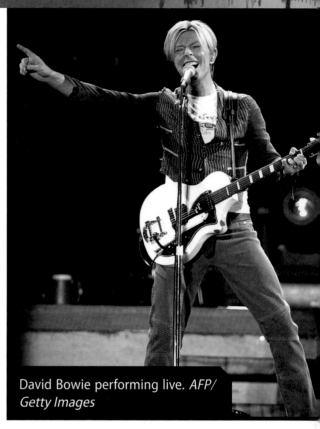

David Bowie performing live. *AFP/ Getty Images*

including one named Davey Jones and the Lower Third. To avoid confusion with Monkees recording star Davy Jones, he changed his name to David Bowie (after the Bowie hunting knife).

In addition to music, Bowie studied painting and mime with a well-known mime troupe, which later influenced his theater work. He also dabbled in Buddhism at a Scottish monastery. By the late 1960s Bowie had formed his own mime troupe, called Feathers. During this time he met American-born Angela Barnett in London. The two were married in 1970 and had a son, Zowie, the following year.

After Bowie's mime troupe broke up he needed capital, so he signed a recording contract and released *Man of Words, Man of Music* (1969), which featured his first hit single, "Space Oddity," a bizarre, haunting tale of a doomed spaceman. His next album, *The Man Who Sold the World* (1970), contained dark, futuristic themes and a cover depicting Bowie decked out in a dress and makeup. Although the album did not fare as well as its predecessor, Bowie suddenly had a cult following on both sides of the Atlantic as king of glitter rock.

In the early 1970s Bowie took over for Marc Bolan as leader of the so-called glam-rock or glitter movement, wearing makeup and extraordinary clothes and leading his band, the Spiders from Mars, under the persona of Ziggy Stardust, an androgynous rock superstar sporting bright henna-red hair and an eye patch. Leaving Ziggy and the band at the height of their success, he began another rapid series of changes. His other personalities during the decade included Aladdin Sane, who wore a lightning bolt across his face and a painted-on teardrop hat, and the Thin White Duke, with slicked-back hair and white suits. Although Bowie's popularity was growing in America, many of his hit singles of this period, such as "Starman" (1972), "The Jean Genie" (1972), "Drive In Saturday" (1973), and "Sorrow" (1973), made the charts only in Britain. "Changes" (1972) made the charts in the United States.

Bowie composed and produced for other artists as well. He boosted rocker Lou Reed's career by producing his hit single "Walk on the Wild Side" (1972), he wrote and produced Mott the Hoople's classic "All the Young Dudes" (1972), and he produced several hit albums for Iggy Pop. By the mid-1970s Bowie had moved to Los Angeles, Calif., where he ventured into feature films. He appeared in Nicolas Roeg's film *The Man Who Fell to Earth* (1976) and had his first American number one hit single with "Fame" (1975), cowritten with John Lennon. Bowie pioneered white Philadelphia soul with *Young Americans* (1975) and moved into more experimental blends of funk, crooned ballads, and electronics for albums like *Station to Station* (1976) and *Low* (1977).

Bowie grew tired of Los Angeles and briefly returned to England before settling into semi-seclusion in Berlin, Germany, where he painted and studied art while trying to end his dependence on drugs. In the late 1970s Bowie hooked up with rocker Brian Eno and collaborated on several avant-garde albums. His eventful life took its toll on his marriage; he and Angela divorced in 1980. Bowie received custody of his son, whom he renamed Joey.

In the early 1980s Bowie was back on top of the charts with his paranoiac *Scary Monsters* album (1980), featuring "Ashes to Ashes," and "Fashion." Bowie subsequently concentrated on his acting career, playing the title role in *The Elephant Man* on Broadway and in Chicago, Ill., and Denver, Colo. In 1981 he collaborated with Queen on their smash hit "Under Pressure." In 1983 Bowie returned to the stage for his first live rock shows in five years, with a world tour that took him from Europe and Britain to the United States and then Japan and Australia. The tour followed the release of his most commercial album up to that time, *Let's Dance* (1983), a confident collection of partly crooned white funk dance songs. The album spawned the hits "China Girl," "Modern Love," and the title track. He also plunged into the burgeoning music video industry and acted in films, including *Merry Christmas, Mr. Lawrence* (1983), *The Hunger* (1983), *Into the Night* (1985), *Absolute Beginners* (1986), and *Labyrinth* (1986).

In the 1990s Bowie continued releasing albums, including the multi-CD retrospective *Singles 1969–1993*, as well as performing live. The multifaceted Bowie married model Iman in 1992, delved into new technologies with *Jump* (1994), a CD-ROM, and appeared as artist Andy Warhol in the feature film *Basquiat* (1996). He was inducted into the Rock and Roll Hall of Fame in 1996.

Bowie's contribution to pop music was his belief in style and change. While the performers of the 1960s had believed in honest self-expression and individualism, Bowie saw himself as the "cracked actor," taking on different roles, personas, and looks and discarding them when they were no longer needed.

JOHANNES BRAHMS

(b. 1833–d. 1897)

T he "three B's" is a phrase often applied to the composers Bach, Beethoven, and Brahms. Johannes Brahms was born in Hamburg, Germany, on May 7, 1833. His father was a double-bass player in a local symphony orchestra. His mother was a seamstress and cook. Johannes was one of three children. At the age of seven he began taking piano lessons. When he was 13 he was already learning musical theory. Brahms was only 15 when he gave his first formal recital.

In 1853, when he was 20, Brahms left home on a concert tour as accompanist to the violinist Eduard Reményi. It was a tour that was to affect the young composer's future enormously. At one of the concerts Brahms met Joseph Joachim, the famous violinist. Joachim was so impressed with the youth's talents that he introduced him to two important musicians—Robert and Clara Schumann. Robert Schumann was a well-known composer, and Clara Schumann, his wife, was a popular concert pianist. The couple took a liking to Brahms, and they also praised the compositions he played for them.

Through an article Schumann wrote about Brahms and his work, the young composer's name became known to important musical circles in Europe. It was largely through Robert's recommendations that the first compositions by Brahms were published. Clara also added to Brahms's growing reputation by playing his music at her recitals.

As his fame spread, Brahms devoted more and more of his time to composing and less to his career as a performer. He continued to hold various musical posts, however. From 1857 to 1859 he was musical director at the German court of Lippe-Detmold. Later, after a brief stay in Hamburg, he became conductor of the Choral Academy in Vienna. In 1872 he held the position of musical director of the Society of the Friends of Music in that city. It was a post he held for three seasons and his last as a full-time conductor. After his resignation he devoted almost all of his time to composing.

Brahms was one of the relatively few composers whose works were fully recognized during their lifetimes. The first of his compositions to bring him fame was his *German Requiem*, which commemorated the death of his mother. He composed more than 300 songs and numerous orchestral, choral, piano, and chamber works. In mid-1896, though seriously ill, he wrote his *Eleven Chorale Preludes* for the organ. Brahms never married. He died in Vienna on Apr. 3, 1897, about a month after his last concert.

JAMES BROWN

(b. 1933–d. 2006)

James Brown was born on May 3, 1933, in Barnwell, S.C. He was raised mainly in Augusta, Ga., by his great-aunt, who took him in at about the age of five when his parents divorced. Growing up in the segregated South during the Great Depression of the 1930s, Brown had an impoverished childhood. Neighbors taught him how to play drums, piano, and guitar, and he learned about gospel music in churches and at tent revivals, where preachers would scream, yell, stomp their feet, and fall to their knees during sermons to provoke responses from the congregation. Brown sang for his classmates and competed in local talent shows but initially thought more about a career in baseball or boxing than in music.

At age 15 Brown and some companions were arrested while breaking into cars. He was sentenced to 8 to 16 years of incarceration but was released after 3 years for good behavior. While in reform school, he formed a gospel quartet. His group, secularized and renamed the Flames (later the Famous Flames), soon attracted the attention of rhythm-and-blues and rock-and-roll shouter Little Richard, whose manager helped promote the group. Intrigued by their demonstration record, a representative of the King record label brought the group to Cincinnati, Ohio, to record for King's subsidiary Federal. Brown's first recording, "Please, Please, Please" (1956), sold three million copies and launched his career. Subsequent hit singles included "I Got You" (1965), "Papa's Got a Brand New Bag" (1965), and "It's a Man's World" (1966). Along with placing nearly 100 singles and almost 50 albums on the charts, Brown broke new ground with two of the first successful "live and in concert" albums—his landmark *Live at the Apollo* (1963), which stayed on the charts for 66 weeks, and his 1964 follow-up, *Pure Dynamite! Live at the Royal*, which charted for 22 weeks.

During the 1960s Brown was known as Soul Brother Number One. His recordings of that decade have often been associated with the emergence of the black power movement, especially the songs "Say It Loud—I'm Black and I'm Proud" (1968), "Don't Be a Drop-Out" (1966), and "I Don't Want Nobody to Give Me Nothing (Open Up the Door, I'll Get It Myself)" (1969). In the 1970s Brown became the Godfather of Soul, and his songs stimulated several dance crazes. When hip-hop music emerged in the 1980s, Brown's songs again assumed center stage as hip-hop disc jockeys frequently incorporated samples (audio snippets) from his records. He also appeared in several motion pictures, including

The Blues Brothers (1980) and *Rocky IV* (1985), and attained global status as a celebrity. Yet Brown's life continued to be marked by difficulties, including the tragic death of his third wife, charges of drug use, and a period of imprisonment for a high-speed highway chase in which he tried to escape pursuing police officers.

A skilled dancer and singer with an extraordinary sense of timing Brown played a major role in bringing rhythm to the foreground of popular music. Brown's ability to "scream" on key, to sing soulful ballads as well as electrifying up-tempo tunes, and to blend blues, gospel, jazz, and country vocal styles made him a highly influential vocalist. His legendary live shows, featuring dramatic entrances and exits, acrobatic leaps, and dazzling footwork, earned him recognition as the Hardest-Working Man in Show Business.

Brown's extraordinary showmanship redefined live performance within popular music and inspired generations of imitators. He proved highly influential also in his innovative use of rhythm. In addition to providing melody and embellishment, the horn players in his bands functioned as a rhythm section (they had to think like drummers), and musicians associated with him (Jimmy Nolan, Bootsy Collins, Fred Wesley, and Maceo Parker) played an important role in defining funk music. Brown was inducted into the Rock and Roll Hall of Fame in 1986. He died on Dec. 25, 2006, in Atlanta, Ga.

JOHN CAGE

(b. 1912–d. 1992)

"Everything we do is music." That is how one of the most inventive American composers of the 20th century described his work. He was John Cage, a minimalist and an avant-garde developer of the percussion orchestra, the prepared piano, the happening, aleatory, or chance, composition, performance art, and music as extended silence. The son of an inventor, John Milton Cage, Jr., was born on Sept. 5, 1912, in Los Angeles, Calif. He attended college briefly and later studied music with Arnold Schoenberg and Henry Cowell. In 1937 Cage organized his own percussion orchestra. As well as more traditional instruments, the group used brake drums, rice bowls, and the jawbone of an ass.

Cage's concert at the Museum of Modern Art in New York City in February 1943 established his reputation as a prominent avant-gardist. His experiments led him to create the prepared piano. He placed various objects, such as nuts, bolts, spoons, clothespins, or strips of rubber, between the strings of a piano to produce percussive and otherworldly sound effects. In the 1940s he also began a professional and personal affiliation with dancer-choreographer Merce Cunningham.

In 1950 Cage began writing pieces that introduced elements of chance. The pitch and duration of sounds were determined by use of charts from the Chinese *I Ching* (Classic of Changes). He also introduced electrically produced sounds, as in *Imaginary Landscape No. 4*, performed with 12 radios with two performers at each, one to change stations and the other the volume.

In 1952 Cage produced his first happening. He composed a score arrived at by chance: a presentation of a lecture, dancing, poetry reading, piano, phonograph records, movie projections, and still paintings—all happening at once. The same year, he composed *4'33"*, a composition consisting of 4 minutes and 33 seconds of silence. Cage continued his musical activities up to his death in New York City on Aug. 12, 1992.

MARIA CALLAS

(b. 1923–d. 1977)

The most exciting opera singer of her generation was the dramatic coloratura soprano Maria Callas. Her voice, with its exceptional expressive powers, was instantly recognizable.

Of Greek parentage, she was born Maria Anna Sofia Cecilia Kalogeropoulo on Dec. 2, 1923, in New York City. In 1937 her family returned to Greece, where she studied voice with Elvira de Hidalgo at the Athens Conservatory. Her first performance was in Athens in 1941. Her appearance in *La Gioconda* by Amilcare Ponchielli at Verona, Italy, on Aug. 2, 1947, was the start of her real career. From 1950 her career

Maria Callas with Tito Gobbi performing in the opera *Tosca. Keystone/Hulton Archive/ Getty Images*

centered at La Scala, the leading opera house in Italy, in Milan. She made her U.S. debut in *Norma* in 1954 at the Lyric Opera of Chicago.

The first singer in 100 years able to perform in the intricate Romantic style and convey tremendous emotional excitement, she became the prime force in the late 20th-century revival of Bellini, Rossini, and Donizetti. Some of her greatest triumphs were in Bellini's *Norma*, Donizetti's *Anna Bolena* and *Lucia di Lammermoor*, Verdi's *Macbeth* and *La Traviata*, and Puccini's *Tosca*.

Although she retired from the operatic stage in 1965, she taught an extensive series of master classes in 1971 and 1972, mostly in New York City. Her final performances took place in 1973 and 1974 in an extensive concert tour of Europe, the United States, and the Far East. She died in Paris on Sept. 16, 1977.

RAY CHARLES

(b. 1930–d. 2004)

Terms such as genius, national treasure, and Father of Soul have been used to describe Ray Charles, a blind African American singer, pianist, bandleader, and composer. He was known for his husky, emotional voice and ability to perform many types of music.

Ray Charles Robinson was born on Sept. 23, 1930, in Albany, Ga. He later dropped the surname to avoid confusion with boxer Sugar Ray Robinson. His family moved to Greenville, Fla., during his infancy. He began losing his sight a few years later and was completely blind by age seven, most likely from glaucoma. Already musically inclined, he perfected his piano skills, learned to play other instruments such as the clarinet, learned to memorize music, and composed scores in Braille at the St. Augustine School for the Blind.

Charles modeled himself after Nat King Cole when he was trying to establish a music career in the late 1940s in bands in Florida and Washington. His earliest recordings included the rhythm-and-blues style "Baby Let Me Hold Your Hand" (1951), the boogie-woogie "Mess Around" (1953), and the novelty song "It Should've Been Me" (1954). During the early 1950s, he also toured with bluesman Lowell Fulson and worked for Guitar Slim, who had a hit with Charles's arrangement of *The Things That I Used to Do* (1953).

Charles drew national attention in the mid-1950s with his stirring performance of "I Got A Woman," a song fusing rhythm and blues, gospel, and jazz. The style was later dubbed soul because of its emotional intensity. He composed or arranged much of what he sang, including "Hallelujah I Love Her So" (1956). The call and response song "What'd I Say?" (1959) gave Charles his first million-seller.

His reputation as a diverse performer grew as he recorded other types of music, including ballads (*The Genius of Ray Charles*, 1959), jazz (*Genius + Soul = Jazz*, 1961), and country (*Modern Sounds in Country and Western*, 1962, featuring the hit "I Can't Stop Loving You"). "Georgia on My Mind," for which Charles won the 1960 Grammy for best male pop vocalist, came from *The Genius Hits the Road* (1960), a concept album containing songs featuring place names. He enjoyed further success on the pop charts with "Hit the Road Jack" (1961).

Charles formed his own band in 1955 and toured extensively for decades, frequently backed by female gospel-style singers known as the Raelettes. Taking greater control of his life in the mid-1960s, he ended his longtime addiction to heroin and formed his own record label, Tangerine (later Crossover). Among his best-known songs of the 1970s were "Living for the City" (1975) and a rendition of "America the Beautiful" (1972). In 1978 he wrote *Brother Ray: Ray Charles' Own Story* with David Ritz.

Charles appeared in the films *Ballad in Blue* (1964) and *The Blues Brothers* (1980), did various guest shots on television shows, and starred in a major advertising campaign (1991–92). In 1987 he endowed the Robinson Foundation for Hearing Disorders. *A Fool for You*, a ballet set to Charles tunes, debuted in 1988. That same year, the National Academy of Recording Arts and Sciences honored him with a lifetime achievement award. He was also recognized by the NAACP Hall of Fame, the Rock and Roll Hall of Fame, and the John F. Kennedy Center for the Performing Arts. He died in Beverly Hills, Calif., on June 10, 2004.

CLIFTON CHENIER

(b. 1925–d. 1987)

American popular musician Clifton Chenier was a pioneer in the development of zydeco music—a bluesy, southern Louisiana blend of French, African American, Native American, and Afro-Caribbean traditions. He was a master keyboard accordionist, a bold vocalist, and the unofficial (but virtually undisputed) "King of Zydeco."

Chenier was born on June 25, 1925, in Opelousas, La., to a family of sharecroppers (tenant farmers) in south-central Louisiana. He spent much of his youth working in the cotton fields. He received his first accordion as a gift from his father, who was an established accordionist in the local house-party (dance) and Saturday-dinner circuit. Chenier immediately recruited a washboard (frottoir) player—his brother Cleveland—to provide the lively, syncopated scraping that has remained a rhythmic hallmark of zydeco music. Inspired by recordings of earlier accordion virtuoso Amadie (or Amédé) Ardoin, as well as by the live performances of many local Cajun and Creole musicians, Chenier quickly became a formidable force in the zydeco tradition.

Chenier left his hometown of Opelousas in his early 20s for Lake Charles in southwestern Louisiana, where he worked for several years as a truck driver for the nearby petroleum companies. During his off-hours he played and listened to music, and his musical style increasingly gravitated toward rhythm and blues. The emblematic features of zydeco—such as the French-based Louisiana Creole language and the ever-popular waltz and two-step dance forms—were never fully excised from his performances, however. In the mid-1950s Chenier signed with Specialty Records, for which he produced mostly rhythm-and-blues recordings with a zydeco tint, notably the hit song "Ay-Tete-Fee" (sung in Louisiana Creole). With his band, the Zodico Ramblers—which, aside from the keyboard accordion and washboard, featured drums, guitar, bass, piano, and saxophone—Chenier emerged as a star of rhythm and blues. His brilliance faded over the next decade, however, and his career remained inert for some years before it was revived and redirected by Arhoolie Records, a label specializing in recordings of regional music traditions. With Arhoolie's support and encouragement, Chenier recalibrated his music back toward its zydeco roots and released a number of successful albums, including *Louisiana Blues and Zydeco* (1965), *King of the Bayous* (1970), and *Bogalusa Boogie* (1975).

Throughout the 1970s Chenier toured nationally and internationally as the King of Zydeco, donning a large gold-and-burgundy mock crown in many of his performances to acknowledge and amplify his popular status. By late in the decade, however, both he and his music had lost their luster; he had developed a severe kidney infection related to diabetes and had to have a portion of his foot amputated. Although Chenier experienced somewhat of a comeback in the early 1980s—when he expanded his band to include a trumpet—his illness continued to take its musical and physical toll, and he ultimately succumbed to it on Dec. 12, 1987.

FRÉDÉRIC CHOPIN

(b. 1810–d. 1849)

Perhaps the greatest of all composers for the piano was Frédéric Chopin. Called a "musical genius" when he was a teenager, Chopin composed a remarkable variety of brilliant pieces—warlike polonaises,

Frédéric Chopin. *Photo Inc/Photo Researchers/Getty Images*

elegant waltzes, romantic nocturnes, and poetic ballades and études.

Frédéric Chopin was born on March 1, 1810, at Żelazowa Wola, a village near Warsaw, Poland. His father, Nicholas, was a Frenchman who had lived in Poland for many years. His Polish mother was of noble birth. Several months after Frédéric's birth the family moved to Warsaw.

Even as a small child, Chopin loved piano music. He began to take piano lessons when he was six years old. He started to compose music even before he knew how to write down his ideas. At the age of eight he performed in a public charity concert. Chopin's first published musical work, a rondo, appeared when he was 15 years old. When Chopin graduated from the lyceum, at 17, he was recognized as the leading pianist of Warsaw and a talented composer.

After Chopin gave two successful concerts in Vienna when he was 19, he began writing works designed for his original piano style. At the same time as his return to Vienna in 1830, Poland revolted against its Russian rulers. The uprising failed, and as a result the Russian czar put Warsaw under harsh military rule. Chopin decided to go to Paris, which was the center of the Romantic movement in the arts. Except for occasional trips, Chopin spent the rest of his life in Paris. He gave lessons and concerts, and publishers paid well for his compositions.

The French loved him for his genius and his charm. Poets, musicians, wealthy Parisians, and Polish exiles were his friends. An important influence was a romantic friendship with Baroness Dudevant, better known as the novelist George Sand. Chopin died of tuberculosis on Oct. 17, 1849, at age 39.

Chopin wrote few concertos and sonatas. Instead he perfected freer musical forms. Among his compositions are some 50 mazurkas, 26 preludes, 24 études, 19 nocturnes, 15 waltzes, 11 polonaises, 4 ballades, and 3 sonatas. For his polonaises and mazurkas he used the rhythms and spirit of Polish folk dances.

ERIC CLAPTON

(b. 1945–)

A multitalented musician, British singer, songwriter, and guitarist Eric Clapton performed rock, pop, and blues as a member of such legendary British bands as Cream and Blind Faith and as a soloist. Clapton's influence as a potent force in the music industry began in the early 1960s and lasted for decades.

Eric Patrick Clapp was born on March 30, 1945, in Ripley, Surrey, England, to Patricia Clapp. He was raised by his grandparents, John and Rose Clapp, who gave him his first guitar as a present. While attending art school in his teens, Clapton became enthralled by such American blues legends as Robert Johnson, Muddy Waters, and Sonny Boy Williamson. In the early 1960s Clapton began jamming in pubs and clubs, substituting as a bandsman for British blues and blues-rock bands. He was a member of the Roosters, a London-based rhythm and blues band, before joining the Yardbirds in 1963. He left the Yardbirds several years later when he decided their music was more pop than blues. He briefly joined John Mayall and his band the Bluesbreakers before hooking up with drummer Ginger Baker and bass player Jack Bruce in 1966 to form Cream. Over the next few years, Clapton and Cream had a number of hits, including "Sunshine of Your Love" and a rocking version of Robert Johnson's "Crossroads." Their 1967 American tour established Clapton's reputation as lead guitarist. His originality and ability to improvise led to his guest recordings with Frank Zappa and the Mothers of Invention

Eric Clapton performing onstage. *Larry Busacca/ Getty Images*

for "We're Only In It for the Money" (1967) and with George Harrison for "While My Guitar Gently Weeps" (1968).

When Cream folded, Clapton and Baker formed Blind Faith in 1969 with Steve Winwood and Rick Grech. Clapton stayed with the group for a year, releasing one album and the hit singles "Can't Find My Way Home" and "Presence of the Lord."

Clapton's self-titled solo debut album (1970) was recorded with his American friends Delaney and Bonnie Bramlett. Later that year, between bouts with alcohol and drug addiction, Clapton assembled yet another group, Derek and the Dominos. Their double album *Layla and Other Assorted Love Songs* (1970) featured the hit single "Layla." Shortly after the release of that album, Clapton, devastated over the loss of two friends—American guitarist and collaborator Duane Allman, who was killed in a motorcycle accident, and guitarist Jimi Hendrix, who died of a drug overdose—retreated into drug use and seclusion.

When Clapton finally shook his addiction he was able to continue his solo career. His second album, *461 Ocean Boulevard* (1974), featuring his version of Bob Marley's hit "I Shot the Sheriff," was followed by a succession of others, which included his classic songs "Wonderful Tonight" and "Lay Down Sally."

In the 1980s, Clapton continued to release outstanding solo albums and began contributing to film sound tracks, beginning with the *Lethal*

Weapon movies. He later scored the films *Rush*, *Back to the Future*, and *The Color of Money*. His retrospective four-CD *Crossroads* (1988) earned him multiple Grammy awards.

Clapton's joy at winning his first Grammy for a single—"Bad Love," from his *Journeyman* (1990) album—was ruined by tragedy when several close friends and road crew members, including Stevie Ray Vaughn, died in a helicopter accident. A worse blow, however, came in 1991 when Conor, his four-year-old son by Italian model Lori Del Santo, fell to his death from a high-rise apartment window. Clapton stopped drinking and wrote one of his most beautiful songs, "Tears in Heaven," in memory of his son. The song was featured on his album *Unplugged* (1992), which topped the charts and swept the Grammy Awards.

Despite his personal tragedies, Clapton continued working, releasing more retrospectives and a blues tribute, *From the Cradle* (1994). He picked up another Grammy in 1997 for his hit single "Change the World" from the feature film *Phenomenon*. In 2000 Clapton was inducted into the Rock and Roll Hall of Fame for the third time when he was recognized for his work as a solo performer. He had previously been inducted as a member of the Yardbirds and Cream.

THE CLASH

Bitish punk rock band the Clash was second only to the Sex Pistols in influence and impact as a standard-bearer for the punk movement. The principal members were Joe Strummer (byname of John Mellor; b. Aug. 21, 1952, Ankara, Turkey–d. Dec. 22, 2002, Broomfield, Somerset, England), Mick Jones (b. Michael Jones; June 26, 1955, London, England), Paul Simonon (b. Dec. 15, 1955, London), Terry ("Tory Crimes") Chimes (b. 1955?, London), and Nick ("Topper") Headon (b. May 30, 1955, Bromley, Kent, England).

Of the many punk bands formed in mid-1970s London as a direct result of the catalytic inspiration of the Sex Pistols, the aptly named Clash came closest to rivaling the Pistols' impact. Their explosive debut single, "White Riot," and first album, *The Clash* (both 1977) were tinny and cranked-up in volume and tempo—the perfect aural signature for scrappy underdogs in stenciled, paint-spattered thrift shop clothes whose credo was "The truth is only known by guttersnipes." Their stage shows were spearheaded by Strummer's teeth-clenched, raw-throated passion.

The Clash was considered so rough, so raw, and so wrong-kind-of-English by the band's American record company that it was not even released in the United States until 1979. Its successor, *Give 'Em Enough Rope* (released in Britain in late 1978 and in the United States in spring 1979), was overseen by American producer Sandy Pearlman in an attempt to capture the American market. However, that breakthrough did not come until the eclectic, sophisticated double album *London Calling* (1980); steeped in reggae and rhythm and blues, it brought the Clash their first American hit single with Jones's composition "Train in Vain (Stand by Me)"—an afterthought added to the album so late that it was not even listed on the cover. By this time the band's hard-won professionalism, rapidly developing musical skills, and increasing fascination with the iconography of classic Americana had distanced them from the punk faithful in Britain, who were still singing along to "I'm So Bored with the U.S.A." from the first album.

Perpetually in debt to their record company and compelled by their punk ethic to give their all for their fans, the Clash tried to satisfy both constituencies with *London Calling's* follow-up, *Sandinista!* (1980), a triple album that unfortunately produced no hits. *Combat Rock* (1982), the last album to feature the classic triumvirate of Strummer, Jones, and Simonon, yielded the hit "Rock the Casbah," which ironically was later appropriated as an American battle anthem during the Persian Gulf War.

Internal tensions brought about by the contradictions within the Clash's stance—between their revolutionary rhetoric and their addiction to the macho posturing of rock stardom—led to the firing of Jones (who went on to found his own group, Big Audio Dynamite). Unfortunately, this left the Clash a very ordinary punk band with an unusually charismatic front man. They recorded one more, poorly received album without Jones and then disbanded in 1986.

Long after the Clash had broken up, their "Should I Stay or Should I Go" became a number one hit in the United Kingdom when it was featured in a commercial in 1991. Despite that success and lucrative offers to reunite, the group refused to do so—unlike the Sex Pistols. One of the Clash's most memorable stage numbers was their version of the Bobby Fuller Four's rockabilly classic "I Fought the Law" (its chorus: "I fought the law / And the law won"); a substitution of the words "the music business" or "capitalism" for "the law" hints at the perennial dilemma for the Clash. However, in its time the Clash pushed its contradictions to the limit and in doing so became for many the most exciting rock band of its era.

PATSY CLINE

(b. 1932–d. 1963)

The life of U.S. country singer Patsy Cline, one of country music's biggest stars, ended abruptly when she died in a plane crash at age 30. At the time of her death, Cline already had a string of top 40 hits and successful concert tours. Her premature death catapulted her to stardom, and her records continued to sell long after her death.

Born Virginia Patterson Hensley on Sept. 8, 1932, in Gore, Va., Patsy began playing piano at age eight and sang duets with her mother in the Gore Baptist Church Choir before she was in her teens. By age 14, she was singing with Joltin' Jim and His Melody Playboys on a Winchester, Va., radio station and soon began singing in local clubs. She married Gerald Cline in 1953 and used her married name professionally. After she won a regional amateur talent contest, she signed a recording contract with Four-Star Records in 1954. In 1955 Cline taped her first recording session for Decca Records at Owen Bradley's studio in Nashville, Tenn.

Cline debuted at the Grand Ole Opry in 1955 singing "A Church, a Courtroom and Then Goodbye," which she later released as a single. The song was appropriately titled, as Cline was soon to divorce her husband. Cline recorded four more songs for Bradley, including "Walkin' After Midnight" (1956), which won first prize when she performed it in 1957 on national television on Arthur Godfrey's *Talent Scouts*. The song was rushed to release and went on to score on both the pop and country charts.

In 1957, Cline married Charlie Dick. The following year the couple had a baby girl, Julia Simadore. Cline and her family relocated to

Nashville, and in 1960 she became a member of the Grand Ole Opry. Finally completing contractual obligations with her former recording company, Cline was now directly under contract with Decca. Her recording of "I Fall to Pieces" (1960) was a turning point in her career, becoming her first number one hit.

Cline gave birth to a son, Randy, in 1961. Later that year, she sustained near-fatal injuries in an automobile accident, though she continued performing and recording, and subsequently released her biggest seller, "Crazy" (1961), written by the then-unknown songwriter Willie Nelson. The following year, Cline had another hit with "She's Got You" (1962). Early in 1963 Cline recorded "Love Letters in the Sand," "Blue Moon of Kentucky," "Sweet Dreams," "Always," and "Crazy Arms." On March 5, 1963, after a benefit performance in Kansas City, Kan., the single-engine plane carrying Cline, her manager, Randy Hughes, and fellow stars Cowboy Copas and Hawkshaw Hawkins crashed near Camden, Tenn., killing all on board. Several months later, "Sweet Dreams" went on to become a posthumous hit.

In 1973, ten years after Cline's death, she became the first female solo performer to be inducted into the Country Music Hall of Fame. Over the years, a number of top-selling collections of Cline's songs were released, as well as tributes from other country performers, including her friend Loretta Lynn. Actress Beverly D'Angelo played Cline in *Coal Miner's Daughter* (1980), the film biography of Loretta Lynn, and Jessica Lange played Cline in *Sweet Dreams* (1985), a feature film based on Ellis Nassour's biography of Cline.

In 1995 a musical entitled *Always...Patsy Cline* opened in Nashville, eventually traveling to other cities as well. With more than six million copies sold, Cline's *Greatest Hits* (1981) attests to the vocalist's enduring popularity.

NAT KING COLE

(b. 1919–d. 1965)

U.S. singer and jazz pianist Nat "King" Cole was born Nathaniel Adams Coles on March 17, 1919, in Montgomery, Alabama. He began playing the organ and the piano in his father's church when he was 12 and made his first recording with the Rogues of Rhythm when he was 19. In 1939 he formed the Nat Cole Trio, and their first hit, "Straighten Up and Fly Right," was recorded in 1943. By 1949 Cole had become an international star, having recorded such hits as "The Christmas Song" and "Unforgettable." After the trio split up Cole launched a solo career, appearing in feature films as well as singing in his trademark husky yet smooth voice. Cole died on Feb. 15, 1965, in Santa Monica, California.

MILES DAVIS

(b. 1926–d. 1991)

The most important jazz bandleader after World War II was Miles Davis. Outstanding among trumpet soloists, he led many small ensembles, including three that were the original sources of major jazz idioms: cool jazz, modal jazz, and fusion.

Born in Alton, Ill., on May 25, 1926, Miles Dewey Davis III grew up in East St. Louis, Ill. His father, a prominent dentist and landowner, gave him a trumpet for his thirteenth birthday, and soon he was playing in local jazz bands. His father, delighted with his talent and determination, sent him to study at what is now the Juilliard School in New York City. Instead of attending classes, he joined Charlie Parker's quintet, developed a simplified bop trumpet style, and performed on many of Parker's greatest recordings. In 1948 Davis formed a nine-piece band to play a new kind of jazz that featured low, muted tone colors. This band, though never commercially successful, was the beginning of cool jazz, which became widespread during the 1950s.

By that time, however, Davis had abandoned cool jazz and was playing a more blues-influenced music, as in his solos on the albums *Bags Groove* and *Walkin'*. He performed with his quintet, which often included tenor saxophonist John Coltrane, and with Gil Evans's big band. Davis began to create music based on the modes, or scales, used by ancient Greek musicians, instead of traditional keys and harmonic patterns. *Kind of Blue* by his sextet in 1959 was the first major modal jazz recording, beginning a

Miles Davis. *Patrick Hertzog/AFP/Getty Images*

trend that remained popular among jazz musicians for the next 10 years.

Davis's jazz quintets of the 1960s, which usually included drummer Tony Williams and tenor saxophonist Wayne Shorter, progressed steadily toward greater harmonic and rhythmic freedom. In 1969 Davis adopted a new approach that combined elements of rock music with jazz, resulting in fusion music. This featured several rhythms played at the same time. His fusion music recordings brought him to the height of his popularity, but in 1975, following a series of severe leg and hip injuries, he retired from performing. He began playing concerts again in 1980, resuming an active touring schedule. He died on Sept. 28, 1991, in Santa Monica, Calif.

CLAUDE DEBUSSY

(b. 1862–d. 1918)

As a child the French composer Claude Debussy was already a rebel. Instead of practicing his scales and technical exercises, the boy would sit at the piano and experiment with different chord combinations. In later years Debussy's unusual chords, based on the whole-tone scale, laid the groundwork for an unconventional style of music called

40

impressionism. He used rich harmonies and a wide array of tone colors to evoke moods, impressions, and images of great subtlety.

Achille-Claude Debussy was born in Saint-Germain-en-Laye, near Paris, on Aug. 22, 1862. When he was seven years old, he began taking piano lessons. When he was nine, his playing attracted Madame Mauté de Fleurville, a former pupil of Frédéric Chopin. Under her tutoring he was able to enter the Paris Conservatory two years later. He won the Grand Prix de Rome in 1884.

Among Debussy's friends were many artists who painted in the impressionist style and poets who wrote in the symbolist style. They too had broken with tradition. Debussy was particularly friendly with the poet Stéphane Mallarmé. It was Mallarmé's poem that inspired Debussy's symphonic poem "Prélude à l'après-midi d'un faune" ("Prelude to the Afternoon of a Faun").

In 1892 Debussy began one of his most notable works, the opera *Pelléas et Mélisande* (*Pelléas and Mélisande*). It was based on a play by Maurice Maeterlinck. Debussy also composed a number of other works in the 1890s. Best known of these was his cycle of Nocturnes for orchestra. They are *Nuages* ("Clouds"), *Fêtes* ("Festivals"), and *Sirènes* ("Sirens"). *Clair de lune* ("Moonlight"), for solo piano, is one of his most popular compositions. His famous *La Mer* ("The Sea"), for orchestra, was first heard in 1905.

Debussy was married twice. For his daughter, Chou-Chou, he wrote the piano work *Children's Corner*. In it is the amusing "Golliwog's Cakewalk." In his last years Debussy was a semi-invalid. Many of his best piano pieces, however, were composed during this period, including his Préludes ("Preludes") and Études ("Studies"). He died in Paris on March 25, 1918.

PLÁCIDO DOMINGO

(b. 1941–)

Beginning with his operatic debut in the 1960s, the Spanish-born tenor Plácido Domingo kept relentlessly active, earning himself

41

a reputation as one of the most versatile, gifted, and charismatic opera singers of his age. He sang more than 100 roles in over 2,700 performances worldwide, made more than 90 recordings, and conducted and directed world-class orchestras. Like his famous predecessor, Enrico Caruso, to whom he was often compared, he embodied the definition of superstar. He attributed his enormous stamina to sheer love of music and opera. Although Domingo was sometimes criticized for diminishing his talent by popularizing it, he was just as often praised for the consistency of his performances, which were characterized by his heroic voice and his dramatic and musical intelligence. His repertoire spanned many styles of music, from late 19th-century Italian and French opera and demanding Wagnerian roles to the popular songs of John Denver, Henry Mancini, and Andrew Lloyd Webber. He was perhaps most famous for his interpretation of the title role of Verdi's opera *Otello*.

Domingo was born on Jan. 21, 1941, in Madrid, Spain, to parents who were noted performers in *zarzuela*, the Spanish operetta form that includes spoken dialogue and satire. While he was still a boy, his parents moved the family to Mexico and founded a company there. Domingo began piano lessons at age eight and won his first competition—a song and dance contest—a year later. He studied briefly at Mexico's National Conservatory of Music before dropping out. Beginning as a baritone, he switched to tenor and made his operatic debut in Monterrey, Mexico, in 1961, singing Alfredo in *La Traviata*. That same year he sang with Joan Sutherland in Dallas, Tex., and with Lily Pons at her farewell performance in Fort Worth, Tex. Thereafter, Domingo's rise to fame was swift. From 1962 through 1965 he was a resident performer at the Tel Aviv Hebrew National Opera, and in 1968 he made his debut at the Metropolitan Opera in New York City, singing Maurizio in *Adriana Lecouvreur* on 35 minutes' notice. In 1969 he sang at La Scala, in Milan.

Domingo was famous for the rapidity with which he learned his roles and the minimal rehearsal time he required to perform. He boasted that as a young man he was able to learn a role in three days. He was also renowned for his ability to sing at a moment's notice. In 1979, while singing *Tosca* in Italy, he flew to Buenos Aires to fill in for a tenor who had fallen ill, flew back to Europe immediately after, and then returned to Buenos Aires to continue his role there. When the San Francisco Opera's 1983 opening night of *Otello* threatened to disintegrate because of another lead tenor's illness, Domingo flew from New York to San Francisco that same night and sang without any rehearsal.

In the 1980s and 1990s, while still flourishing as a singer, Domingo began to explore other facets of his talent. In 1983 he wrote his autobiography, *My First Forty Years*. In 1984 he became artistic consultant to the Los Angeles Music Center Opera; over the years, he conducted, sang, helped shape the repertory, and made casting decisions. Domingo's passion for music led him to develop new roles and to perform operas that had often been neglected for many years. He promoted the music of Hispanic composers and used his Spanish background to advantage when interpreting these works. At the Los Angeles Opera he directed a production of Manuel Penella's *El Gato Montes* and at the Bonn Opera, *Il Guarany* by the Brazilian Carlos Gomes. In 1992 he helped direct the musical program for the Seville International Festival, and in 1993 he established an annual world singing competition, the Operalia.

By far the best known of all of Domingo's concerts were the Three Tenors concerts in which he sang popular operatic arias and other songs with Luciano Pavarotti and José Carreras. After their first appearance in Rome in 1990, the three repeated their hugely successful performance in Los Angeles' Dodger Stadium in 1994 and again in 1996 and 1997 for a worldwide tour. These televised productions reached over a billion viewers, and though critics often chided Domingo for cheapening his talent, he was also credited for bringing opera into the lives of people who would never have experienced it otherwise.

Domingo also ventured into conducting, taking the podium for the Vienna State Opera, the Los Angeles Music Center Opera, and the Metropolitan Opera in New York City. His 1997 concerts conducting the Chicago Symphony Orchestra with Daniel Barenboim at the piano attracted much attention and huge crowds. However, his conducting was never as well received as his singing and was often criticized as shallow and undeveloped.

In the 1990s Domingo expanded his repertory yet again, performing in more Wagnerian operas, including *Die Walküre* and *Parsifal*. He also sang Mozart's *Idomeneo* and the role of Count Ipanov in the rarely staged *Fedora* by Umberto Giordano. In 1996 he became director of the Washington Opera. Working with Leonard Slatkin, he staged a lauded production of *Pagliacci* by Ruggero Leoncavallo. In the same year he opened a restaurant called Domingo in New York City. By 1997 he had sung over 400 performances at the Metropolitan Opera and showed no signs of slowing down. When asked about his future goals, he stated that one of his ambitions was to sing or record every Verdi role. Beloved by his fans and unflagging in his energy and commitment to music, Domingo earned his reputation as an icon of 20th-century opera.

BOB DYLAN

(b. 1941–)

From the early 1960s Bob Dylan was one of the most influential—and at times controversial—performers in American music. He was known for his trademark nasal vocals and scores of compositions that were often made popular by other performers, including "Blowin' in the Wind" and "Mr. Tambourine Man." He reinvented the folk music genre, along the way affecting pop, rock, and country with his poetic and often political songs.

Born Robert Alan Zimmerman on May 24, 1941, in Duluth, Minn., Dylan grew up in the mining town of Hibbing, Minn., to which he moved with his family at age six. Although at one time he told tales of having been a rebellious child who often ran away from home, Dylan later disavowed such stories. In reality he lived a fairly normal, middle-class childhood, during which he developed a love of music that inspired him to take up guitar, harmonica, and piano. Dylan formed a rock and roll band, the Golden Chords, as a freshman in high school. He briefly attended the University of Minnesota, where he began performing in coffeehouses as Bob Dylan, a name he took in honor of poet Dylan Thomas. He legally adopted the name several years later.

Dylan moved to New York in the early 1960s. Following his first live appearance at a Greenwich Village folk club, he landed a record contract. Although his debut album, *Bob Dylan* (1962), failed to reach the charts, it created a sensation with its raw renditions of traditional folk songs. His second album, *The Freewheelin' Bob Dylan* (1963), featured his own compositions and included two anti-war anthems, "A Hard Rain's Gonna Fall" and "Blowin' in the Wind." The latter became a huge hit for the folk trio Peter, Paul, and Mary.

By 1964 Dylan was per-

Bob Dylan. *Express Newspapers/Hulton Archive/ Getty Images*

forming 200 concerts a year. With "The Times They Are A-Changin'" (1964), "Subterranean Homesick Blues" (1965), "Mr. Tambourine Man" (1965), and "Maggie's Farm" (1965), Dylan began mixing protest songs with personal music while adding blues and rock and roll to his mix. Dylan's songs often became huge hits for other performers, including the Byrds with "Mr. Tambourine Man," the Turtles with "It Ain't Me Babe," and Cher with "All I Really Want to Do." Touring with Levon Helm, Robbie Robertson, and the Band, Dylan recorded his first million-selling single, "Like a Rolling Stone" (1965). The following year he released "Rainy Day Woman #12 & 35," his second platinum single, and "Just Like a Woman." By 1966 Dylan's worldwide sales exceeded 10 million.

After a serious motorcycle accident in 1966, Dylan went into temporary seclusion. He released the apocalyptic "All Along the Watchtower," then re-emerged in the late 1960s with mellow country-influenced songs such as "Lay Lady Lay" (1969). Through the early 1970s Dylan toured with the Band and collaborated with such artists as Beatle George Harrison, with whom Dylan cowrote "I'd Have You Anytime" and "If Not for You."

In 1973 Dylan scored a hit with "Knockin' on Heaven's Door" from the film *Pat Garrett and Billy the Kid*. He earned his first platinum album with *Desire* (1976), which featured the hit singles "Hurricane" and "Mozambique." Dylan performed with the Rolling Thunder Revue, a large, evolving group that included Joan Baez, Roger McGuinn, Ramblin' Jack Elliott, and poet Allen Ginsberg. Following a complicated divorce from his wife, Sara Lowndes, and an extensive world tour, Dylan declared himself a born-again Christian in the late 1970s.

In the 1980s Dylan recorded and performed with a variety of artists, including Tom Petty, Mark Knopfler, Eric Clapton, George Harrison, Roy Orbison, Mick Taylor, and even reggae stars. He appeared in a feature film, *Hearts of Fire* (1987), which was generally panned. *Oh Mercy* (1989) is considered his best album of the decade.

Dylan was inducted into the Rock and Roll Hall of Fame in 1988. In 1990 he was awarded France's highest cultural award. He received a lifetime achievement award at the 1991 Grammy Awards. During the 1990s Dylan released numerous anthologies and retrospectives, was honored at a 30th-anniversary all-star gala at New York's Madison Square Garden, appeared at the 1994 Woodstock festival, and toured with one of his strongest bands ever. In 1997 he received the Kennedy Center Honors, the highest award for distinction in the performing arts bestowed in the United States, and was chosen to play for Pope John Paul II at a religious congress in Bologna, Italy. After years of mediocre record sales, the phenomenal success of Dylan's 1997 release, *Time Out of Mind*, earned him two Grammy Awards and confirmed his status as a living legend. He won another Grammy for his 2001 release, *Love and Theft*.

In 2003 Dylan cowrote and starred in the film *Masked and Anonymous*. The next year he released what many saw as the first in a series of autobiographies, *Chronicles: Volume 1. No Direction Home*, a documentary directed by Martin Scorsese, appeared on television in 2005 and was widely praised by critics. A sound track album that included 26 previously unreleased tracks came out before the documentary aired. In 2006 Dylan became the host of the weekly *Theme Time Radio Hour* and released his 44th album, *Modern Times*, which won the 2007 Grammy Award for best contemporary folk album. He also received an award for best solo rock vocal performance for "Someday Baby." In 2009 he released his 33rd studio album, *Together Through Life*, which debuted at the top of the British and American album charts.

Dylan's later honors included Spain's Prince of Asturias Prize for the Arts in 2007 and a special citation in 2008 from the Pulitzer Prize Board for his "profound impact on popular music and American culture." In 2012 he was awarded the U.S. Presidential Medal of Freedom.

DUKE ELLINGTON

(b. 1899–d. 1974)

The A Train, part of the New York City subway system, ran to north Manhattan's Harlem area. There, one could find the Cotton Club, a white-owned nightclub for white audiences but featuring African American entertainers. From 1927 to 1932 Duke Ellington was closely associated with the Cotton Club, so there is little wonder that his signature tune became "Take the A Train," composed by his long-time collaborator, pianist Billy Strayhorn. A jazz pianist, composer, and bandleader, Ellington was one of the most eminent and creative U.S. musicians of the 20th century. The range of his accomplishments was so great over a 55-year career that his impact on music has yet to be assessed adequately.

Edward Kennedy Ellington was born in Washington, D.C., on Apr. 29, 1899. Although he showed considerable artistic talent as a youth, he turned down a scholarship to devote himself to music. He was largely a self-taught pianist. By his teens he was influenced by the ragtime composers of the era. In about 1918 he formed a band to play local engagements, and by 1923 he was in New York City leading a small band at the Kentucky Club.

From there Ellington went to the Cotton Club, where his band included such jazz greats as Johnny Hodges, Barney Bigard, and Cootie

Williams. This period and the years that followed brought him and his band international recognition for such compositions as "Mood Indigo," "Sophisticated Lady," "I Got It Bad and That Ain't Good," "Solitude," "Satin Doll," and "Black and Tan Fantasy." Appearances on the Broadway stage and concert tours of the United States and Europe further enhanced their reputation.

In 1943 a longer Ellington piece, *Black, Brown, and Beige*, premiered at Carnegie Hall. He wrote *Liberian Suite* in 1947 for the centennial of Liberia. He was commissioned by Arturo Toscanini in 1950 to write *Harlem* for the NBC Symphony Orchestra. A later aspect of his career was religious jazz, compositions to be performed at worship services. In 1969 he was awarded the Presidential Medal of Freedom. Ellington died on May 24, 1974, and the band passed to the leadership of his son, Mercer.

EMINEM

(b. 1972–)

U.S. rapper, record producer, and actor, Eminem was known as one of the most controversial and best-selling artists of the early 21st century. A white performer who had won acceptance in an art form dominated by African Americans, Eminem was revered by some critics but reviled by others. Some accused him of misogyny and homophobia. Arguably, he became one of pop music's most controversial figures.

Marshall Bruce Mathers III was born on Oct. 17, 1972, in St. Joseph, Mo. He had a turbulent childhood, marked by poverty and allegations of abuse. At age 14 Mathers began rapping in clubs in Detroit, Mich., and, when unexcused absences kept him in the ninth grade for the third year, he quit school, determined to make it in hip-hop music. As Eminem, he made a name for himself in the hip-hop underground, but his first album, *Infinite* (1996), sold poorly, and he continued to work menial jobs.

When Eminem placed second in the freestyle category at the 1997 Rap Olympics in Los Angeles, he came to the attention of Dr. Dre, founding member of pioneering rappers N.W.A. and the head of Aftermath Entertainment. By this time Eminem had developed the persona of the inhibitionless Slim Shady, who gave voice to Eminem's id in often vulgar and violent lyrics. With Dr. Dre as his producer and mentor, Eminem released *The Slim Shady LP* early in 1999. Benefiting from the inventive channel-surfing music video for the hit song "My Name Is" and the instant credibility of Dr. Dre's involvement, the album went multiplatinum, and Eminem won two Grammy Awards and four MTV Video Music Awards.

Grounded in his life experience but seemingly reflecting a troubled psyche, Eminem's songs outraged many, including the Gay & Lesbian Alliance Against Defamation, which denounced him as a homophobic misogynist. His tumultuous relationship with his wife, Kim, was chronicled in songs in which he rapped about killing her. In 2000 Eminem was charged with assault when he allegedly pistol-whipped a man he saw kissing her; the couple divorced in 2001, and their relationship remained rocky (in 2006 the couple remarried and divorced again). His mother also sued him for defaming her in song and in interviews.

In 2000 Eminem released *The Marshall Mathers LP*—the fastest-selling album in the history of rap. The incredible success of the album brought more controversy. To silence critics, in 2001 Eminem performed a duet with openly gay musician Elton John at the Grammy Awards, where *The Marshall Mathers LP* was nominated for best album of the year. Later that year he recorded the album *Devil's Night with D12* (also known as the Dirty Dozen), a Detroit-based rapping sextet, and toured with the group. He also created his own record label, Shady Records. The D12 collective, 50 Cent, and other rappers signed to and released albums with the label.

When he finished touring in 2002, Eminem made his acting debut in the semiautobiographical *8 Mile*. The gritty film was a critical and commercial success. The following year he won an Academy Award for "Lose Yourself," a song featured in the movie. Eminem's later works include *The Eminem Show* (2002) and *Encore* (2004). While both albums proved successful, neither brought Eminem the attention garnered by his previous two. In 2005 he issued a greatest-hits set—*Curtain Call: The Hits*—that topped the charts. Eminem then stepped out of the public eye, resurfacing briefly in 2006 to eulogize friend and D12 member Proof, who was killed outside a Detroit nightclub.

In 2008 Eminem published the memoir *The Way I Am*, which included photos, drawings, and lyrics. The following year he released *Relapse*, his first collection of new material in five years. While it featured solid production from Dr. Dre, the album met with middling reviews because of its over-the-top attempts to shock and its somewhat dated catalog of pop culture references. Nevertheless, *Relapse* won the 2010 Grammy Award for best rap album, and Eminem shared the Grammy for best rap duo or group with Dr. Dre and 50 Cent for the single "Crack a Bottle." Eminem's 2010 release *Recovery* was a response to the criticisms leveled at *Relapse*, and it was his sixth album to top the Neilsen SoundScan chart for weekly sales. At the 2011 Grammy Awards Eminem repeated in the best rap album category, winning for *Recovery*, and the album's lead single, "Not Afraid," was honored for best rap solo performance.

ELLA FITZGERALD

(b. 1918–d. 1996)

Composer Ira Gershwin once said, "I never knew how good our songs were until I heard Ella Fitzgerald sing them." Such praise was often bestowed upon the "First Lady of Song," a musical legend whose clear, sweet voice glided between low and high notes.

Ella Fitzgerald was born on Apr. 25, 1918, in Newport News, Va., and grew up primarily in Yonkers, N.Y. Winning a talent contest at Harlem's Apollo Theater at age 16 brought her to the attention of Chick Webb. She began performing in his band in 1935 and took over as its leader upon Webb's death in 1939. She made her first recording, "Love and Kisses," in 1935 and had a million-seller in 1938 with "A-Tisket, A-Tasket," a song for which she helped write the lyrics.

Fitzgerald embarked on a solo career during the 1940s. From the latter part of the decade through the mid-1950s, she toured with impresario Norman Granz's show *Jazz at the Philharmonic*. During this time, her mastery of scat—turning the voice into an instrument by using nonsense syllables to improvise to the music—came through in songs such as "Flying Home," "How High the Moon," and "Oh, Lady Be Good."

Granz became Fitzgerald's personal manager and producer. Under his guidance, in 1956 she began recording the *Songbooks*, a series of albums celebrating the works of notable U.S. composers and lyricists. The collection covered some 250 songs; albums focused individually on Cole Porter, Richard Rodgers and Lorenz Hart, Duke Ellington, George and Ira Gershwin, Irving Berlin, Harold Arlen, Jerome Kern, and Johnny Mercer.

When the National Academy of Recording Arts and Sciences began presenting Grammy Awards in 1958 Fitzgerald was honored for *Ella Fitzgerald Sings the Irving Berlin Songbook*. She continued to dominate the category of best pop vocal performance by a female for several years, winning in 1959 for "But Not for Me", in 1960 for *Mack the Knife—Ella in Berlin*, and in 1962 for *Ella Swings Brightly with Nelson Riddle*. She also was honored several times in jazz categories. In 1967 she received the Trustees Award for Lifetime Achievement.

Known for a willingness to experiment, Fitzgerald included ballads, jazz, bossa nova, show tunes, novelty numbers, and Beatles songs in her repertoire. She recorded more than 100 albums during her lengthy career and performed with such artists as Louis Armstrong, Count Basie, and Oscar Peterson. She appeared on television in the U.S. and abroad some 200 times, and her movie credits included *Pete Kelly's Blues* (1955), *St. Louis Blues* (1958), and *Let No Man Write My Epitaph* (1960).

Fitzgerald continued to record and perform in the 1970s and 1980s despite an eye problem that required her to wear very thick glasses. She had open-heart surgery in 1986 but returned to show business until diabetes forced doctors to amputate her legs below the knee in 1993. She died on June 15, 1996, in Beverly Hills, Calif.

ARETHA FRANKLIN

(b. 1942–)

U.S. singer Franklin defined the golden age of soul music of the 1960s. In 1987 she became the first woman inducted into the Rock and Roll Hall of Fame.

Aretha Franklin. *Walter Iooss Jr./Hulton Archive/Getty Images*

Aretha Louise Franklin was born on March 25, 1942, in Memphis, Tenn. Aretha's mother, Barbara, was a gospel singer and pianist. Her father, C.L. Franklin, presided over the New Bethel Baptist Church of Detroit, Mich., and was a minister of national influence. A singer himself, he was noted for his brilliant sermons, many of which were recorded by Chess Records.

Her parents separated when she was six, and Aretha remained with her father in Detroit. Her mother died when Aretha was 10. As a young teen, Aretha performed with her father on his gospel programs in major cities throughout the country and was recognized as a vocal prodigy. Her central influence, Clara Ward of the renowned Ward Singers, was a family friend. Other gospel greats of the day—Albertina Walker and Jackie Verdell—helped to shape young Franklin's style. Her album *The Gospel Sound of Aretha Franklin* (1956) captures the electricity of her performances as a 14-year-old.

At age 18, with her father's blessing, Franklin switched from sacred to secular music. She moved to New York City, where Columbia Records executive John Hammond, who had signed Count Basie and Billie Holiday, arranged her recording contract and supervised sessions highlighting her in a blues-jazz vein. From that first session, "Today I Sing the Blues" (1960) remains a classic. But, as her Detroit friends on the Motown label enjoyed hit after hit, Franklin struggled to achieve crossover success. Her record label placed her with a variety of producers who marketed her to both adults ("If Ever You Should Leave Me," 1963) and teens ("Soulville," 1964). Without targeting any particular genre, she sang everything from Broadway ballads to youth-oriented rhythm and blues. Critics recognized her talent, but the public remained lukewarm until 1966, when she switched to Atlantic Records, where producer Jerry Wexler allowed her to sculpt her own musical identity.

At Atlantic, Franklin returned to her gospel-blues roots, and the results were sensational. "I Never Loved a Man (the Way I Love You)" (1967) was her first million-seller. Surrounded by sympathetic musicians playing spontaneous arrangements and able to devise the background vocals herself, Franklin refined a style associated with Ray Charles—a rousing mixture of gospel and rhythm and blues—and raised it to new heights. As a civil-rights-minded nation lent greater support to black urban music, Franklin was crowned the Queen of Soul. "Respect," her 1967 cover of Otis Redding's spirited composition, became an anthem operating on personal and racial levels. "Think" (1968), which Franklin wrote herself, also had more than one meaning.

In the early 1970s she triumphed before an audience of flower children at the Fillmore West in San Francisco and on whirlwind tours of Europe and Latin America. Her return to church music, *Amazing Grace* (1972), is considered one of the greatest gospel albums of any era. By the late 1970s disco cramped Franklin's style and eroded her popularity. But in 1982, with help from singer-songwriter-producer Luther Vandross, she was back on top with a new label, Arista, and a new dance hit, "Jump to It," followed by "Freeway of Love" (1985).

GEORGE AND IRA GERSHWIN

George Gershwin: (b. 1898–d. 1937)
Ira Gershwin: (b. 1896–d. 1983)

One of the first composers to use jazz themes within classical music forms, George Gershwin was primarily involved in the Broadway musical theater. Ira Gershwin, his brother, worked with him, writing the words to his music in more than 20 stage musicals and motion pictures. Their *Of Thee I Sing* was the first musical to win a Pulitzer Prize (1932).

George Gershwin was born on Sept. 26, 1898, in Brooklyn, N.Y., the son of Russian immigrants whose name had been Gershovitz. He began studying piano at age 12, and at 16 he quit high school to work as a piano-playing song plugger for a music publishing company. His first song was published in 1916, and two years later his "Swanee" was popularized by the singer Al Jolson. The first musical for which Gershwin wrote all the music was *La La Lucille*, produced in 1919. From 1920 to 1924 he wrote dozens of songs for the annual show *George White's Scandals*, attracting the attention of its bandleader, Paul Whiteman. In 1924 Whiteman commissioned Gershwin to write a short composition for a jazz concert. The result was *Rhapsody in Blue*, which became one of his most acclaimed works.

Also in the year 1924 the Gershwin brothers achieved their first major Broadway success—*Lady Be Good*. This was their first full-scale collaboration, and the beginning of one of the most successful song-writing teams in Broadway history. They produced, among others, "Tip-Toes" (1925), "Oh, Kay!" (1926), "Strike Up the Band" (1927; revised 1930), "Funny Face" (1927), and "Girl Crazy" (1930).

Many people will agree that the most ambitious Gershwin work is the opera *Porgy and Bess* (1935). It is based on the novel *Porgy* by DuBose Heyward, who joined Ira in writing the libretto. Although it was originally called a stage show and later a folk opera, inspiring much controversy with its innovative use of jazz and related themes, it has taken its place as a genuine American opera.

Long after his initial success as a composer, George studied with the then avant-garde composers Henry Cowell and Wallingford Riegger and the theorist Joseph Schillinger. Gershwin's "serious" compositions include *Piano Concerto in F* (1925), a set of preludes for piano (1926), the tone poem "An American in Paris" (1928), and *Second Rhapsody* for piano and orchestra (1931). He began writing for motion pictures just before his death in Hollywood, Calif., on July 11, 1937. A film on his life, *Rhapsody in Blue*, appeared in 1945.

Ira Gershwin was born in New York City on Dec. 6, 1896. He attended City College of New York for two years and did odd jobs until his collaboration with his younger brother, George. Among their enduring love songs were "Someone to Watch Over Me" and "Embraceable

You." The last score completed by the brothers was for the film "A Damsel in Distress" (1937). Among the composers Ira worked with after George's death was Harold Arlen, on the musical remake of "A Star Is Born" (1954). His career continued until his death in Beverly Hills, Calif., on Aug. 17, 1983, while rewriting lyrics for Gershwin tunes used in the musical comedy *My One and Only*.

GILBERT AND SULLIVAN

William Schwenck Gilbert: (b. 1836–d. 1911)
Arthur Sullivan: (b. 1842–d. 1900)

For more than a century the comic operas of William S. Gilbert and Arthur Sullivan have delighted audiences all around the world. Between 1871 and 1896 they created words and music for 13 operas. Although they worked well together, they were characteristically unalike. Gilbert wrote the words for their operas. His amusing, hilarious rhymes and tricks of phrasing added color, variety, and vigor to his topsy-turvy plots. Sullivan wrote the music. His lighthearted tunes have been hummed, whistled, and played ever since.

William Schwenck Gilbert was first a government clerk, then a lawyer, and finally a dramatist. He was born on Nov. 18, 1836, in London. While at Ealing School he wrote several student dramas. He attended King's College. The verses he wrote while studying law, first published in papers and magazines, were collected in two books, *Bab Ballads* and *More Bab Ballads*. Until he collaborated with Sullivan, he was a successful but not an outstanding dramatist.

Arthur Seymour Sullivan was Victorian England's most famous composer of popular and sacred songs and oratorios. Sullivan was born in London on May 13, 1842, the son of a poor Irish musician. As a boy he was a soloist with the Chapel Royal choristers. His superior talents won him scholarships at the Royal Academy of Music in London and at the Leipzig Conservatory in Germany. "The Tempest," based on the Shakespearean play, won him fame before he was 20. "Onward! Christian Soldiers" is his best-known hymn; "The Lost Chord" is one of his songs.

The two met in 1870. Within a year their first opera, *Thespis*, was performed. It was not successful: they did not rejoin efforts until 1875. Then they created *Trial by Jury*, which made fun of the judiciary. They had written it for Richard D'Oyly Carte. Within three years he formed the famous D'Oyly Carte Company to produce Gilbert and Sullivan operas.

Their most successful operas are: *The Sorcerer* (1877); *H.M.S. Pinafore* (1878); *The Pirates of Penzance* (1879); *Patience* (1881); *Iolanthe* (1882), thought to be their finest; *The Mikado* (1885), their biggest success; *The Yeoman of the Guard* (1888); and *The Gondoliers* (1889). After *The Gondoliers* the partners quarreled furiously over who should pay for carpeting their theater, the Savoy.

Gilbert's caricatures of government and officials angered Queen Victoria. She knighted Sullivan in 1883. Gilbert had to wait for Edward to ascend the throne before he was knighted in 1907. Sullivan died on Nov. 22, 1900; Gilbert, on May 29, 1911.

PHILIP GLASS

(b. 1937–)

American composer Philip Glass wrote instrumental, vocal, opera, ballet, and film music so distinctive that it cannot be easily labeled. It has been called both avant-garde and postmodern. Although his music was judged as too simplistic by some critics and too unconventional for mainstream appeal by others, later in his career he achieved broad critical acclaim and popularity, especially for his operas and film scores.

Glass was born in Baltimore, Md., on Jan. 31, 1937. He developed a fondness for chamber music while working in his father's record shop. At the age of eight he began to study flute at the Peabody Conservatory. He entered the University of Chicago when he was 15 and graduated with degrees in mathematics and philosophy. Next he attended the Juilliard School, earning a master's degree in 1962. Later, with a Fulbright grant, Glass went to Paris to study with Nadia Boulanger. His early works show the influence of Arnold Schoenberg, Anton von Webern, and Alban

Berg, as well as of Indian classical music. Elements of rock and jazz are also evident. The climax of his early minimalist period was *Music in 12 Parts* (1974). In musical composition, minimalism is characterized by extreme simplicity, and it often has a repetitive or symmetrical quality.

Glass wrote several symphonies as well as concertos and chamber, piano, and choral music. After the success of his trilogy of "portrait operas"—*Einstein on the Beach* (1976), *Satyagraha*, based on the life of Mahatma Gandhi (1980), and *Akhnaten* (1984)—he received numerous commissions for new

Philip Glass. *AFP/Getty Images*

works. His more than 20 operas include *White Raven* (1991), *The Voyage* (1992), *Galileo Galilei* (2001), *Appomattox* (2007), and works based on the writing of Doris Lessing, Franz Kafka, and Allen Ginsberg and the films of Jean Cocteau. He also wrote scores for several films, including *Koyaanisqatsi* (1982), *Kundun* (1997), and *The Hours* (2002).

BENNY GOODMAN

(b. 1909–d. 1986)

At the height of the swing era, the King of Swing was U.S. clarinetist and bandleader Benny Goodman. It was Goodman's orchestra that established the most popular big-band jazz style of the 1930s and brought a new level of recognition to jazz. Along with recording a string of hit songs, he also introduced several other top jazz and popular music performers.

Benjamin David Goodman was born on May 30, 1909, in Chicago, Ill. He received his first music training in 1919 at a Chicago synagogue, and the following year he played in bands and took lessons at Jane Addams' Hull House. He studied with German classical instructor Franz Schoepp and absorbed jazz basics through jam sessions with Chicago-area musicians. In 1926 Goodman joined the Ben Pollack jazz band and made his first solo recording, "He's the Last Word." He lived in New York City from 1929 and worked as a studio musician, performing on more than 1,000 recordings. In 1933–34 he formed his own big band that played regularly on *Let's Dance*, a late-night network radio program. In May 1935, he took his band on a tour of the United States that was a failure until he reached the Palomar Ballroom in Los Angeles in August. There, crowds of enthusiastic young dancers and fans of *Let's Dance* greeted the band, and the swing era in popular music began.

From this point, the Goodman band went on to unprecedented heights of fame. The band's hits during its early years included "Don't Be That Way," "Stompin' at the Savoy," and "Goody Goody," as well as the band's two theme songs "Let's Dance" and "Goodbye." The group became a favorite of white audiences while playing orchestrations by outstanding black arrangers, especially Fletcher Henderson. Goodman also pioneered racial integration in his jazz trio (1935–36), quartet (1936–39), and sextet (1939–41), featuring black musicians, including Teddy Wilson (piano), Lionel Hampton (vibraphone), and Charlie Christian (guitar). Band members Harry James (trumpet) and Gene Krupa (drums) and singer Peggy Lee also rose to fame while working with Goodman. In pioneering the small group, or chamber jazz ensemble, Goodman made what is perhaps his most important contribution to jazz history.

The Goodman orchestra performed at Carnegie Hall in New York City with guest artists from the bands of Duke Ellington and Count Basie in January 1938. The recording of the highly successful evening has been released several times and is heralded as one of the greatest albums of live jazz. Goodman reorganized his band in the 1940s and brought in new talent and arrangers, including Eddie Sauter and Mel Powell, who took the band in a more modern direction. As the 1940s progressed, the bop movement began to replace swing music, and Goodman broke up his band. He intermittently led small and big bands during the 1950s and recorded in the traditional, classical swing style. In 1955 he recorded the sound track for *The Benny Goodman Story*, a movie loosely based on his life. In 1962 he took a jazz band to the Soviet Union on a U.S. State Department tour. He went on to appear occasionally in special concerts, on world tours, and as a clarinetist with symphonic orchestras and smaller groups. Goodman died on June 13, 1986, in New York City.

As a jazz soloist, Goodman's playing was a refined version of earlier Chicago-based jazz clarinet styles. At a time when it was unusual for a jazz musician also to play classical music, he played works by Mozart and others. He recorded with the Budapest String Quartet and commissioned works by the contemporary composers Béla Bartók, Paul Hindemith, and Aaron Copland.

GUIDO D'AREZZO

(b. 990–d. 1050)

A rezzo's principles served as a foundation for modern Western musical notation. Educated at the Benedictine abbey at Pomposa, Guido evidently made use of the music treatise of Odo of Saint-Maur-des-Fossés and apparently developed his principles of staff notation there. He left Pomposa in about 1025 because his fellow monks resisted his musical innovations, and he was appointed by Theobald, bishop of Arezzo, as a teacher in the cathedral school and commissioned to write the *Micrologus de disciplina artis musicae*. The bishop also arranged for Guido to give (*c.* 1028) to Pope John XIX an antiphonary he had begun in Pomposa.

Born around 990 in Arezzo, Italy, Guido d'Arezzo seems to have gone to the Camaldolese monastery at Avellana in 1029, and his fame developed from there. Many of the 11th-century manuscripts notated in the new manner came from Camaldolese houses.

The fundamentals of the new method consisted in the construction by thirds of a system of four lines, or staff, and the use of letters as clefs. The red F-line and the yellow C-line were already in use, but Guido added a black line between the F and the C and another black line above the C. The neumes could now be placed on the lines and spaces between and a definite pitch relationship established. No longer was it necessary to learn melodies by rote, and Guido declared that his system reduced the 10 years normally required to become an ecclesiastical singer to a year.

Guido was also developing his technique of solmization, described in his *Epistola de ignoto cantu*. There is, however, no evidence that the Guidonian hand, a mnemonic device associated with his name and widely used in the Middle Ages, had any connection with Guido d'Arezzo.

Guido is also credited with the composition of a hymn to St. John the Baptist, *Ut queant laxis*, in which the first syllable of each line falls on a different tone of the hexachord (the first six tones of the major scale); these syllables, ut, re, mi, fa, sol, and la, are used in Latin countries as the names of the notes from c to a (ut was eventually replaced by do). His device was of immense practical value in teaching sight-reading of music and in learning melodies. Singers associated the syllables with certain intervals; mi to fa, in particular, always represented a half step.

Before Guido an alphabetical notation using the letters from a to p was used in France as early as 996. Guido's system used a series of capital letters, small letters, and double small letters from a to g. Guido's system also came to be associated with the teaching of the gamut—the whole hexachord range (the range of notes available to the singer).

In addition to his innovations Guido also described a variety of *organum* (adding to a plainchant melody a second voice singing different pitches) that moved largely, but not completely, in parallel fourths. Guido's work is known through his treatise the *Micrologus*.

WOODY GUTHRIE

(b. 1912–d. 1967)

The most famous of the more than 1,000 songs he wrote is "This Land Is Your Land," a composition taken up as an anthem by the civil rights and anti-Vietnam movements of the 1960s. By the time of his early death, Woody Guthrie had become the most legendary of modern American folksingers. His son Arlo and associates such as Pete Seeger have helped keep his music and memory alive.

Woodrow Wilson Guthrie was born in Okemah, Okla., on July 14, 1912. His schooling ended in 10th grade, and he left home at 15 to wander the country by freight train. Carrying with him his guitar and harmonica, Guthrie became a welcome figure in the hobo and migrant camps of the Great Depression of the 1930s. He was close to the struggles of the common people, and their experiences were reflected in his songs. He became a musical spokesman for working people in songs such as "So Long (It's Been Good to Know Yuh)," "Hard Traveling," "Blowing Down this Old Dusty Road," "Union Maid," and "Tom Joad" (inspired by John Steinbeck's novel *The Grapes of Wrath*).

In New York City he joined Pete Seeger and others in the Almanac Singers, who

Woody Guthrie. *Library of Congress Prints and Photographs Division*

performed mostly for farmer and worker groups. After service in the Merchant Marine during World War II, he returned to the group and wrote a series of songs and sketches entitled "American Folksongs." The last years of his life were spent in a New York hospital fighting Huntington's chorea, a disease of the nervous system that took his life on Oct. 3, 1967.

GEORGE FRIDERIC HANDEL

(b. 1685–d. 1759)

A musical giant of the late baroque period, George Frideric Handel was born in Germany but spent most of his adult life in England. He successfully combined German, French, Italian, and English musical styles in about 40 operas, 20 oratorios, and numerous other vocal pieces, instrumental works, and church music.

Handel was born on Feb. 23, 1685, in Halle, Brandenburg. In addition to studying music, he was trained in law at Halle University. Although appointed organist of the Halle Cathedral in 1702, he moved to Hamburg the next year, where he obtained a position as violinist, and later harpsichordist, in the opera orchestra. His *St. John Passion* was performed in 1704 and his first opera, *Almira*, in 1705.

Handel then went to Italy, which was the musical center of Europe, where his work was already known. He met the leading musicians of the day and composed the operas *Rodrigo* and *Agrippina*, many Italian solo cantatas, Latin church music, and the oratorio *La Resurrezione*.

In 1710 Handel succeeded his friend Agostino Steffani as director of music for the elector of Hanover. A few months later he left for London. His opera *Rinaldo* was received enthusiastically in London in 1711, and his *Ode for the Queen's Birthday* and *Utrecht Te Deum and Jubilate* in celebration of the Treaty of Utrecht in 1713 won him a royal pension.

As composer, producer, and director of operas, Handel continued until 1741 despite changing public tastes, backstage rivalries, and financial problems. In 1718 he became director of music to the duke of Chandos, for whom he composed the *12 Chandos Anthems* and *Haman and Mordecai*, later reworked as *Esther*, the beginning of a string of oratorios that continued until 1752 with *Jephtha*. His famous *Messiah* was written for a performance in Dublin, Ireland, in 1742.

Among Handel's most popular works are the orchestral suites *Water Music* (1717) and *Music for the Royal Fireworks* (1749), both for wind and string band. He also composed about 80 overtures and was one of the great masters of the *concerto grosso*, in which a small group of soloists contrasts with the full orchestra.

After recovering from several periods of poor health, Handel began to have trouble with his eyes in 1751. Two years later he was nearly blind. He died on Apr. 14, 1759, and was buried in Westminster Abbey.

W.C. HANDY

(b. 1873–d. 1958)

William Christopher Handy was born on Nov. 16, 1873, in Florence, Ala., the son of former slaves. Handy was a son and grandson of Methodist ministers, and he was educated at Teachers Agricultural and Mechanical College in Huntsville, Ala. Going against family tradition, he began to cultivate his interest in music at a young age and learned to play several instruments, including the organ, piano, and guitar. He was a particularly skilled cornetist and trumpet player.

Longing to experience the world beyond Florence, Ala., Handy left his hometown in 1892. He traveled throughout the Midwest, taking a variety of jobs with several musical groups. He also worked as a teacher in 1900–02. He conducted his own orchestra, the Knights of Pythias from Clarksdale, Miss., from 1903 to 1921. During the early years of this period of his life, Handy was steeped in the music of the Mississippi Delta and of Memphis, and he began to arrange some of those tunes for his band's performances. Unable to find a publisher for the songs he was beginning to write, Handy formed a partnership with Harry Pace and founded Pace & Handy Music Company (later Handy Brothers Music Company).

Handy worked during the period of transition from ragtime to jazz. Drawing on the vocal blues melodies of African American folklore, he added harmonizations to his orchestral arrangements. His work helped develop the conception of the blues as a harmonic framework within which to improvise. With his "Memphis Blues" (published 1912) and especially his "St. Louis Blues" (1914), he introduced a melancholic element, achieved chiefly by use of the "blue" or slightly flattened seventh tone of the scale, which was characteristic of African American folk music.

Later he wrote other blues pieces ("Beale Street Blues," 1916; "Loveless Love") and several marches and symphonic compositions. He issued anthologies of African American spirituals and blues (*Blues: An Anthology*, 1926; *W.C. Handy's Collection of Negro Spirituals*, 1938; *A Treasury of the Blues*, 1949) and studies of black American musicians (*Negro Authors and Composers of the United States*, 1938; *Unsung Americans Sung*, 1944). His autobiography, *Father of the Blues*, was published in 1941.

JOSEPH HAYDN

(b. 1732–d. 1809)

Called the father of both the symphony and the string quartet, Joseph Haydn founded what is known as the Viennese classical school—consisting of Haydn, his friend Mozart, and his pupil Beethoven. He lived from the end of the Baroque period to the beginning of the Romantic and presided over the musical transition between them. His distinct style combined elements of the Baroque, the gallant style from Italy and France, and the emotional *empfindsamer Stil*, or "sensitive style," of the north Germans.

Franz Joseph Haydn was born on March 31, 1732, in Rohrau, Austria. When he was seven he entered the choir school of St. Stephen's Cathedral in Vienna. He composed avidly but had no formal training until his late teens, when he worked with the Italian Niccolò Porpora. In 1761 Haydn was engaged by the Esterházy family, and until the death in 1790 of Prince Miklós József Esterházy, Haydn directed an orchestra, choir, and opera company. At the Esterháza castle Haydn composed a continuous stream of works for performance. His fame spread throughout Europe, and his works were published, but he tired of the confinement. Prince

Miklós's successor, however, cared nothing for music, and Haydn was suddenly free.

The impresario Johann Peter Salomon offered Haydn a contract for 12 new pieces to be performed in London. Haydn was lionized in London, and he stayed for 18 months, returning again in 1794. His two sets of symphonies known as the *Salomon*, or *London* (Nos. 93–104), and the six *Apponyi Quartets* are among his greatest works.

He returned to Vienna in 1795, and his late oratorios—*The Creation*, first performed in 1798, and *The Seasons* (1801)—were finally successful with the Viennese public. Haydn died in Vienna on May 31, 1809. His enormous output includes 107 symphonies, about 50 divertimenti, 84 string quartets, about 58 piano sonatas, and 13 masses, among numerous other works.

FLETCHER HENDERSON

(b. 1897–d. 1952)

Henderson was an American musical arranger, bandleader, and pianist who was the leading pioneer in the sound, style, and instrumentation of big band jazz.

Fletcher Henderson was born on Dec. 18, 1897, in Cuthbert, Ga., into a middle-class family; his father was a school principal and his mother a teacher. He changed his name (James was his grandfather's name, Fletcher Hamilton his father's) in 1916 when he entered Atlanta University, from which he graduated as a chemistry and math major. In 1920 he moved to New York, intending to work as a chemist while pursuing a graduate degree. Although he found a part-time laboratory job, he immediately began getting work as a pianist. Within months he was a full-time musician, and he began working for W.C. Handy's music publishing company as a song plugger, promoting songs to performers. In 1921 he took a position as musical factotum for Black Swan records, the first black-owned recording company, for which he organized small bands to provide backing for such singers as Ethel Waters. He played piano for leading black singers on more than 150 records between 1921 and 1923 and then began a full-time career as a bandleader.

Although Henderson had shown an interest in music from child-hood, when his mother taught him piano, he knew little about jazz until he was in his twenties. His orchestra, made up of well-established New York musicians, at first played standard dance-band fare, with occasional ragtime and jazz inflections. The band became more jazz-oriented in 1924 when Henderson hired the young trumpeter Louis Armstrong. At about the same time, the band's musical director and alto saxophonist, Don Redman, conceived the arrangements and instrumentation that would become the standard for big bands. The rhythm section was established as piano, bass, guitar, and drums; and the trumpet, trom-bone, and reed sections composed the front line. Arrangements were constructed in the call-and-response manner (e.g., the brass section "calls," the reed section "responds"), and many tunes were based upon "riffs," identifiable musical passages repeated throughout the song. After Redman left the band in 1927, Henderson used the same approach in his own arrangements.

Henderson was a superb arranger, but he was a poor businessman. Although the band had played major venues and been heard on the radio and in recordings, the band's finances were frequently in disarray, and musicians often left without notice to join other bands. He nevertheless managed to keep his band going until the mid-1930s, at which time he sold many of his arrangements to Benny Goodman, who used them to define the sound of his new band. "King Porter Stomp," "Down South Camp Meetin'," "Bugle Call Rag," "Sometimes I'm Happy," and "Wrappin' It Up" are among the Henderson arrangements that became Goodman hits.

Through the Goodman band, Henderson's arrangements became a blueprint for the sound of the swing era. (Other arrangers, including Henderson's brother Horace, also contributed to the big band sound of the 1930s.) Henderson arranged for Goodman for several years and formed a short-lived band of his own in 1936 that included Roy Eldridge, Chu Berry, John Kirby, and Sid Catlett. That year, Henderson issued "Christopher Columbus," which became the biggest hit released under his own name. Henderson had little success in his subsequent attempts to organize bands and spent most of the 1940s arranging for Goodman, Count Basie, and others. He formed a sextet in 1950 that became the

house band at New York's Cafe Society, but he suffered a stroke soon thereafter and was forced to retire.

JIMI HENDRIX

(b. 1942–d. 1970)

O ne of the most influential performers in the history of rock, Jimi Hendrix earned legendary status with his mastery of the electric guitar. Although Hendrix's wild, innovative instrumentals were widely imitated by scores of later rock musicians, his talent remained unparalleled.

Johnny Allen Hendrix (he was renamed James Marshall Hendrix by his father at age four) was born on Nov. 27, 1942, in Seattle, Wash., to Al Hendrix, an African American, and his wife, Lucille, a Cherokee. At age 16 Hendrix purchased his first acoustic guitar. Being left-handed, Hendrix turned the guitar upside down and taught himself to play by imitating blues legends Muddy Waters, B.B. King, and rock legend Chuck Berry. Hendrix played with local bands throughout high school and enlisted in the Army following graduation, only to be discharged several years later after suffering injuries from a parachuting accident.

Using the pseudonym Jimmy James, Hendrix returned to music. He toured the country, working as a pick-up artist for such acts as Sam Cooke, Little Richard, Curtis Mayfield, and Ike and Tina Turner. In 1964 Hendrix moved to New York and began playing the club circuit with the Isley Brothers. Two years later, he formed his own group, Jimmy James and the Blue Flames. During a performance in Greenwich Village he was discovered by former Animals bassist Chas Chandler, who offered to manage him. Chandler convinced Hendrix to accompany him to London, where Hendrix teamed up with drummer Mitch Mitchell and bass player Noel Redding. Hendrix soon changed his name to Jimi, and formed the Jimi Hendrix Experience.

The trio's debut single, "Hey Joe," was an immediate hit, and it was followed by "Stone Free." He had two more top-ten hits with "Purple Haze" and "The Wind Cries Mary." The following year, the Experience performed in clubs in England, France, Belgium, and West Germany.

The cover of the Jimi Hendrix Experience's debut album *Are You Experienced. Michael Ochs Archives/ Getty Images*

Hendrix's debut album, *Are You Experienced* (1967), a mix of psychedelic blues, acid rock, and Hendrix's raw vocals, was first released in the United Kingdom. In June 1967 the Experience made its United States debut at the Monterey International Pop Festival in California. Hendrix's fabled performance at that concert included playing his guitar with his teeth and then setting it on fire. Later that year the Experience embarked on a brief American tour with the Monkees, but Hendrix's outrageous stage antics did not go over well with the Monkees' teenybopper audience.

Hendrix spent the next few years touring Britain and the United States. Audience reception was mixed: the band was alternately cheered and booed. In 1968, at the height of his commercial and critical success, Hendrix released *Axis: Bold as Love* (1968) and *Electric Ladyland* (1968). Additional hit singles from this period included "Foxy Lady," "Purple Haze," a cover of Bob Dylan's "All Along the Watchtower," "Burning of the Midnight Lamp," and "Voodoo Chile."

Following an incendiary performance at Woodstock in 1969, in which he performed "The Star-Spangled Banner," simultaneously coaxing from his electric guitar the sounds of bombs falling and machine gun fire, the Jimi Hendrix Experience broke up, due in part to increasing personal, business, and drug problems. Pressured by black leaders to remain part of the music scene, Hendrix formed another group, the Band of Gypsys, which was also short-lived. In January 1970, during a concert before 19,000 fans at New York City's Madison Square Garden, Hendrix walked out in the middle of his second number.

Years of drug and alcohol abuse, coupled with the pressures of nonstop touring, eventually took its toll. Hendrix died of accidental suffocation in a drug-related incident on Sept. 18, 1970, in his girlfriend's London apartment. Close to a hundred albums of Hendrix's music have been released posthumously, a testimony to the public's unending interest in Hendrix the artist and the rock icon. Jimi Hendrix was posthumously inducted into the Rock and Roll Hall of Fame in 1992.

BILLIE HOLIDAY

(b. 1915–d. 1959)

Lady Day, as Billie Holiday was usually called, was the finest jazz singer of her generation, and in the opinion of her followers and many critics she was the greatest jazz singer of the 20th century. The 1956 autobiography of Billie Holiday written in collaboration with William Dufty and the movie made from it in 1972 were both called *Lady Sings the Blues*. The title is less a reflection of her music than of her unhappy childhood and the struggle against heroin addiction later in her life. Although Holiday received no professional training, her singing was sophisticated and her diction and phrasing were dramatically intense.

Billie Holiday was born Eleanora Fagan on Apr. 7, 1915, in Baltimore, Md. Her parents were unwed teenagers, Sadie Fagan and Clarence Holiday. Her father was a professional guitarist. Young Holiday made her singing debut in 1931 in obscure Harlem nightclubs. Her first recording session, with accompaniment by Benny Goodman, was held in 1933. She was not widely recognized until 1935, but her early recordings are now regarded as jazz masterpieces.

Although she was still singing in 1958, Holiday's best years were from 1936 to 1943, when her professional and private relationship with saxophonist Lester Young created some of the finest recorded examples of the interplay between vocal and instrumental music. (It was Young who first called her Lady Day.) She appeared in concert with Duke Ellington, Count Basie, Fletcher Henderson, Benny Goodman, Chick

Webb, Artie Shaw, and others. Among the compositions associated with her are "Strange Fruit," "Fine and Mellow," "Yesterday's," "God Bless the Child," "Don't Explain," "Lover Man," and "Gloomy Sunday." Holiday died in New York City on July 17, 1959.

BUDDY HOLLY

(b. 1936–d. 1959)

U.S. musician Buddy Holly was an outstanding singer, songwriter, and guitarist of the 1950s who produced some of the most distinctive and influential work in rock-and-roll music. Holly and his musical group, the Crickets, recorded such rock classics as "That'll Be the Day," "Rave On," "Peggy Sue," and "Oh Boy." Holly's career ended prematurely when he died, along with singers Richie Valens and the Big Bopper (J.P. Richardson), in a plane crash at Mason City, Iowa, on Feb. 5, 1959.

Charles Hardin Holley (the "e" was dropped from his last name—probably accidentally—on his first record contract) was born in Lubbock, Tex., on Sept. 7, 1936, the youngest of four children in a family of gospel-loving, devout Baptists. He became seriously interested in music at about age 12 and pursued it with remarkable natural ability. The African American rhythm and blues that Holly heard on the radio had a tremendous impact on him, and by age 16, he became a rhythm-and-blues devotee. By 1955, after hearing Elvis Presley, Holly was a full-time rock and roller. Late that year he bought a Fender Stratocaster electric guitar and developed a style of playing featuring ringing major chords that became his trademark. In 1956 he signed with Decca Records's Nashville, Tenn., division, but the records he made for them sold poorly and were uneven in quality. His first break came and went quickly.

In 1957 Holly and his new group, the Crickets, began their association with independent producer Norman Petty at his studio in Clovis, N.M. Together they created a series of recordings that displayed an emotional intimacy and sense of detail that set them apart from other 1950s rock and roll. When the Crickets' first single, "That'll Be the Day," was released in 1957, their label, Brunswick, did nothing to promote it. Nevertheless, the record had an irrepressible spirit, and by year's end it became an international multimillion-seller. Soon after, Holly became a star and an icon.

Holly and the Crickets' association with Petty (who, in addition to being their producer, served as their manager, songwriting partner, and publisher , and owned their recordings) was far from all beneficial, however. According to virtually all accounts, he collected the Crickets' royalty checks and kept the money. By 1959 the hit records tapered off, and Holly was living in New York with his new bride. Estranged from the Crickets and broke, he was

Buddy Holly. *Hulton Archive/Getty Images*

also contemplating legal action against Petty. This left him little choice but to participate in the Winter Dance Party of 1959 tour through the Midwest, during which he and co-headliners Ritchie Valens and the Big Bopper were killed in a plane crash. In 1986 Holly was posthumously inducted into the Rock and Roll Hall of Fame, and in 1996 he was honored by the National Academy of Recording Arts and Sciences with a lifetime achievement award.

CHARLES IVES

(b. 1874–d. 1954)

At a time when most other United States composers were following European traditions, Charles Ives was creating a uniquely American music. His works, unknown and unplayed during most of his lifetime, contained many innovations associated with 20th-century music. These innovations include polytonality (the simultaneous use of, usually, two tonalities, often creating great dissonance) and polyrhythms (conflicts of rhythm, or cross rhythms)—both identified with Igor Stravinsky; and atonality (the total absence of a tonal center)—associated with Arnold Schoenberg.

Charles Edward Ives was born on Oct. 20, 1874, in Danbury, Conn. His father was an unorthodox musician given to experimentation. From him Ives gained an appreciation for natural sounds—church bells, crowds—as well as for popular music—hymns, marches, dance tunes— all of which later figured prominently in his music. As a young boy he learned to play the piano, violin, cornet, drums, and organ.

Ives continued to study music at Yale University, where he produced conventional works. After graduating, Ives chose a business career, feeling that his music would be stronger and better if he did not depend on it for a living. He helped establish a successful insurance business, but his free time was devoted to music. Ill health limited his output after 1917, and he ceased composing in 1926. He retired from his business in 1930 and moved to Connecticut. He died in New York City on May 19, 1954.

Ives wrote his music not for the public or for critics but to satisfy his own creative urge. In 1920 he published his monumental "Concord Sonata" for piano and in 1922 his "114 Songs," both distributed privately to friends. The piano sonata was not performed publicly until 1939. It was not until the late 1920s, when the composer Henry Cowell printed some of Ives's pieces in his "New Music," that Ives's music attracted attention. "Three Places in New England" for orchestra was in 1931 given the first major performance of any of his works. His "Third Symphony," written between 1901 and 1911, was not performed until 1946. In 1947 he won the Pulitzer Prize for this work, though he characteristically refused the award. The "Second Symphony" was written between 1897 and 1902, but the piece was not performed in its entirety until 50 years after its composition. The first complete performance of the "Fourth Symphony" was conducted by Leopold Stokowski—11 years after the composer's death.

Ives's early organ work, "Variations on America" (1891–94), is the earliest known piece using polytonality. This and the orchestral "New England Holidays" (1904–13) have become relatively popular. "The Unanswered Question," which was composed sometime before 1908, is one of the earliest examples of chance, or aleatoric, music—music in which indeterminate elements are left for the performer to improvise.

MAHALIA JACKSON

(b. 1911–d. 1972)

With her booming, soulful voice, African American singer Mahalia Jackson belted out hymns and spirituals with an intensity and richness that made her famous around the world. Although she could have become a successful blues singer, Jackson decided at an early age to devote her talent to music with religious content and her energy to helping people live in peace and harmony.

Mahalia Jackson was born on Oct. 26, 1911, in New Orleans, La., to Johnny Jackson, a longshoreman, preacher, and barber, and his wife, Charity, a laundress and maid. A very poor family, the Jacksons were also extremely religious. Mahalia's mother, who died when Mahalia was five, was a devout Baptist, and Mahalia regularly sang hymns in the church choir. Growing up in New Orleans, Mahalia was also influenced by the diverse sounds and rhythms of the streets, as well as the songs of legendary blues singer Bessie Smith. While the blues style was popular with blacks in the South, Mahalia's family rejected blues songs as being decadent and discouraged her from singing them.

When she was 16, Jackson went to live with a relative in Chicago, where she hoped to attend nursing school. Armed with only an eighth-grade education, Jackson soon found herself earning money doing domestic work. Upon joining a local Baptist church, Jackson auditioned for the choir and was immediately invited to be a soloist. Word of her talent spread and soon she was performing at other churches and at funerals throughout the Chicago area. When Jackson's grandfather had a stroke and lapsed into a coma, she promised that if he recovered she would never sing any songs of which he would disapprove. He recovered and she kept her vow, though she was later offered large sums of money to perform the blues in nightclubs.

Beginning in the late 1930s, Jackson spent five years touring the country with well-known composer Thomas A. Dorsey. They visited churches and gospel tents, where Jackson would sing traditional hymns. Having earned very little money in her years of touring, Jackson returned to Chicago and opened a beauty shop and a flower shop. One day Jackson was practicing in a recording studio in 1946 when a Decca record company representative overheard her singing and asked her to make a recording. "Move on up a Little Higher" (1946) became her breakthrough hit. The single eventually went platinum and thrust her into the national spotlight.

Suddenly famous, Jackson bought an automobile large enough to sleep in so that she would have a place to spend the night when she performed in segregated areas where motels refused rooms to blacks. She also carried her own food with her so that she would not have to patronize segregated restaurants. Jackson's remarkable singing eventually attracted white audiences. Her popularity spread nationally and internationally. One of Jackson's most famous concerts took place in Israel, where she performed for an audience of Christians, Jews, and Muslims.

Jackson devoted a great deal of her time and energy to the civil rights movements of the 1950s and 1960s. She participated in the Montgomery bus boycott that followed Rosa Parks's refusal to give up her bus seat to a white person. She sang the old inspirational "I Been 'Buked and I Been Scorned" to more than 200,000 people at the 1963 march on Washington, D.C., just before Martin Luther King's famous "I Have a Dream" speech.

Jackson died from heart failure on Jan. 27, 1972, and was mourned by fans around the world. Her one unfulfilled ambition had been to build a nonsectarian, nondenominational church in Chicago. Mahalia Jackson was inducted into the Rock and Roll Hall of Fame in the Early Influences category in 1997.

MICHAEL JACKSON

(b. 1958–d. 2009)

World renowned as the "King of Pop," U.S. singer, songwriter, producer, and dancer Michael Jackson was among the most popular entertainers in the music industry in the early and mid-1980s. Capitalizing on the advent of music videos, Jackson electrified audiences everywhere with his trademark dance moves showcased in clips accompanying the hit singles, "Thriller," "Beat It," and "Billie Jean"—which featured his signature "moonwalk" dance.

Michael Joseph Jackson was born on Aug. 29, 1958, in Gary, Indiana, to parents Katherine and Joseph Jackson. The seventh of nine children in a musically talented family, Michael, at the age of five, joined his four older brothers to form a vocal pop music group known as the Jackson 5. Encouraged by their father, Joseph, the Jackson 5 soared to stardom after signing a recording contract with Motown Records, becoming one of the most acclaimed musical families known to rock and roll. At age 11, Michael made his first national television appearance, exhibiting the talent and charm that would eventually catapult him to superstardom as a solo artist. He soon became the leading vocalist of the group.

As a member of the Jackson 5, Michael began his solo performance career with the release of his first single, "Got To Be There" in 1971. The following year marked the release of Michael's first number one solo single, "Ben," which was the title song from a film about a favorite pet rat. Another hit single, "Rockin' Robin," reached number two on the pop charts. The Jackson 5 continued to record hit songs for Motown through 1975, after which they signed a new recording contract with Epic Records as the Jacksons. By the end of the 1970s, however, Michael began to pursue his own solo career with the new recording company.

Jackson's first solo album for Epic, called *Off the Wall* (1979), became the best-selling album of the year and remained in the top ten for eight months. It became the first album in history to produce four top ten singles. Two of those singles, "Don't Stop 'til You Get Enough" and

Michael Jackson. *Lee Celano/AFP/Getty Images*

"Rock with You," became international, number one hits and were certified gold records. In 1982, Jackson released his megahit *Thriller*, which became the biggest-selling solo album of all time—selling more than 40 million copies. It won numerous awards, including an unparalleled eight Grammy Awards, and was certified platinum the following year. The album featured seven top-ten hits, including the number one hit singles, "Thriller," "Billie Jean," and "Beat It." Another hit single included an easygoing duet with Paul McCartney called "The Girl Is Mine," which reached number one on the rhythm-and-blues charts, as well as number two on the pop charts. The following year, the award-winning music video/ short film *Thriller* debuted on MTV. Jackson's second solo album, *Bad* (1987), the long-awaited follow-up to *Thriller*, produced seven hit singles, including the title track, "Man in the Mirror," and "Dirty Diana." Jackson released his third solo album, *Dangerous*, in 1991, which featured the hit single and video, "Black or White." Other album releases included, *HIStory: Past, Present, and Future, Book I* (1995), a collection of 15 old and 15 new tracks, and *Blood on the Dancefloor: HIStory in the Mix* (1997), which contained eight remixes from the previous album, plus five new songs. A collection of new material was offered on *Invincible* in 2001. In addition to his own recording Jackson found the time to write and produce successful records for other artists including "Muscles" (1982) for Diana Ross and "Centipede" (1984) for his sister Rebbie.

Aside from recording music, Jackson was involved with several other projects during the course of his career. In 1978, he played the part of the scarecrow in the musical film *The Wiz*. He reunited with his brothers to tour the United States and Canada in 1984 with the Victory reunion tour. Jackson, along with Lionel Richie wrote "We Are the World" in 1985 to benefit the U.S.A. for Africa famine relief operation. Jackson and Richie recorded the song with several other popular artists of the day. In 1988, Jackson published his autobiography, entitled *Moonwalk*, which was subsequently adapted into a film.

Jackson's eccentric, secluded lifestyle grew increasingly controversial in the early 1990s. His reputation was seriously damaged in 1993 when he was accused of child molestation by a 13-year-old boy he had befriended; a civil suit was settled out of court. In 1994 Jackson secretly married Lisa Marie Presley, daughter of Elvis Presley, but their marriage lasted less than two years. Shortly thereafter Jackson married again, this marriage producing children, though it, too, ended in divorce. While he remained an international celebrity, his image in the United States was slow to recover, and it suffered even more in November 2003 when he was arrested and charged with child molestation. After a 14-week trial that became something of a media circus, Jackson was acquitted in 2005. Jackson was inducted into the Rock and Roll Hall of Fame as a member of the Jackson 5 in 1997 and as a solo performer in 2001.

In 2009, Jackson began rehearsals for a series of comeback concerts billed as the This Is It tour. During rehearsals, Jackson died suddenly on June 25, 2009, in Los Angeles, Calif., from cardiac arrest following intoxication from medications administered under his personal physician's care. His physician was subsequently convicted of involuntary manslaughter, while memorials, a documentary titled *Michael Jackson's This Is It*, and an album *Number Ones,* caused a resurgence in his popularity worldwide.

JAY-Z

(b. 1970–)

Since the 1990s, U.S. rapper and entrepreneur Jay-Z has become one of the most influential figures in hip-hop music. Shawn Corey Carter

Jay-Z. *Adam J. Sablich/Shutterstock.com*

was born on Dec. 4, 1970, in Brooklyn, N.Y. He grew up in Brooklyn's often dangerous Marcy Projects, where he was raised mainly by his mother. His first-hand experience with illicit drug dealing influenced his lyrics when he began rapping under the stage name Jazzy, soon shortened to Jay-Z (a name that may also have been derived from the proximity of the J and Z subway lines to the Marcy Projects). Jay-Z and two friends founded their own company, Roc-a-Fella Records, to release his debut album, *Reasonable Doubt* (1996), which climbed the Billboard charts, reaching number 23 on the pop chart and number 3 on the rhythm-and-blues chart.

A string of successful albums followed at a rate of at least one per year through 2003. *Vol. 2... Hard Knock Life* (1998) not only was the first of Jay-Z's releases to top the Billboard 200 album sales chart but also won a Grammy Award for best rap album. In 2001 he pleaded guilty to assault relating to a 1999 nightclub stabbing and received three years' probation. In 2003, with the release of *The Black Album*, Jay-Z announced his retirement as a performer. In 2004 he assumed the presidency of Def Jam Recordings, making him one of the most highly placed African American executives in the recording industry at the time.

Postretirement, Jay-Z stayed remarkably active, collaborating with the rock group Linkin Park in 2004 and appearing as a guest vocalist on the recordings of numerous other artists, including Kanye West and Beyoncé. He developed a large portfolio of business ventures and investments, including Roc-a-Fella Films, a clothing line, and a stake in the New Jersey Nets of the National Basketball Association. Jay-Z formally returned to recording in 2006 with *Kingdom Come*. In Dec. 2007 he stepped down as Def Jam president shortly after releasing the album *American Gangster*.

Jay-Z proved that he remained one of rap's most bankable acts when he embarked on a highly successful tour with singer Mary J. Blige in 2008. The following year he won a Grammy Award for best rap performance for "Swagga Like Us," a collaboration with T.I., Kanye West, and Lil Wayne, and that September he released *The Blueprint 3*, which featured guest vocals from Alicia Keys and production by West and Timbaland. The album continued to generate Grammy-winning singles for more than a year, with "Run This Town," a collaboration with Rihanna and West, and "D.O.A. (Death of Auto-Tune)" being honored in 2010 and "Empire State of Mind," a collaboration with Keys, and "On to the Next One" scoring wins in 2011. Jay-Z continued his streak of Grammy success in 2012, winning best rap performance for "Otis," a single from *Watch the Throne* (2011), an ambitious and highly regarded collaboration with West. The following year he won three additional Grammy Awards; best rap performance and best rap song for "N****s in Paris," and along with West and featuring Frank Ocean and The-Dream, he won best rap/sung collaboration for "No Church in the Wild." In 2010 Jay-Z published a memoir, *Decoded*. He is married to fellow artist Beyoncé.

ROBERT JOHNSON

(b. 1911–d. 1938)

A frican American blues musician Robert Johnson is considered by many to be the finest blues artist of all time.

Born May 8, 1911, in Hazlehurst, Miss., into the large family of a sharecropper, Johnson grew up in Memphis, Tenn. He was sent as a child to live with his mother's husband, Charles Dodds, who lived in Memphis. When he learned that his real father was Noah Johnson, he took Johnson as his name. He received little education but learned to play the harmonica. Johnson was influenced by Son House and other musicians with whom he came in contact in the South. He perfected his slide guitar, thematic lyrics, and emotionally intense vocals while traveling from town to town playing in juke joints. Myth had it that Johnson, called the King of the Delta Blues, sold his soul to the devil in exchange for superior guitar playing ability.

Johnson traveled and played music throughout the southern United States. Johnson had only two recording sessions (1936–37), both for the American Record Company, which were rereleased in 1990 by Columbia as *Robert Johnson: The Complete Recordings*. He was a pioneer in slide guitar and in bottleneck. His recordings never became big commercial successes but were influential in bringing Mississippi Delta-style blues into the mainstream. Such songs as "Preachin' Blues," "Come On in My Kitchen," "Me and the Devil Blues," and "Hellhound on My Trail" influenced such later blues stars as Muddy Waters and Eddie Taylor. His other classic compositions include "Sweet Home Chicago," "Dust My Broom," and "Ramblin' on My Mind." Johnson died on Aug. 16, 1938, in Greenwood, Miss. He was inducted into the Blues Foundation's Hall of Fame in 1980 and into the Rock and Roll Hall of Fame in 1986.

JOSQUIN DES PREZ

(b. *c.* 1440–d. 1521)

A Flemish composer now considered the greatest of the Renaissance, Josquin was also widely acclaimed in his own lifetime. His full name takes many forms.

Josquin was born about 1440 in the province of Hainaut, now in Belgium, possibly at Condé-sur-L'Escaut. He was probably a chorister at the collegiate church of St. Quentin and was a singer from 1459 to 1472 in the cathedral at Milan, Italy. He then served Duke Galeazzo Maria Sforza in Milan and later in the papal chapel. Before becoming choirmaster of the chapel of Ercole I d'Este, Duke of Ferrara, in 1503, he seems to have been associated with the chapel of Louis XII of France and with the cathedral of Cambrai. At the duke's death in 1505, Josquin became provost of the collegiate church of Notre Dame in Condé, where he spent the remainder of his life.

Twenty of his masses survive in their entirety. Of these, 17 were printed in his lifetime, as were many motets and chansons. He developed methods inherited from the late Middle Ages, using imitative and antiphonal techniques.

Martin Luther admired his music, calling him a "master of the notes, which must do as he wishes; other composers must do as the notes wish." Josquin was also praised for his teaching. He died at Condé on Aug. 27, 1521.

B.B. KING

(b. 1925–)

Reared in the Mississippi Delta, guitarist B.B. King was a principal figure in the development of blues music. With his influence on rock as well as blues musicians, he helped broaden the appeal of the blues.

Riley B. King was born on Sept. 16, 1925, in Itta Bena, near Indianola, Miss. The earliest influence on his singing was gospel music that he heard in church. To his own impassioned vocal calls, King played distinctive, single-string guitar responses; his guitar style was influenced by T-Bone Walker, by Delta blues players (including his cousin Bukka White), and by such jazz guitarists as Django Reinhardt and Charlie Christian. He worked for a time as a disc jockey in Memphis, Tenn., where he acquired the name B.B. (for "Blues Boy") King. In 1951 he made a hit record of "Three O'Clock Blues," which led to virtually

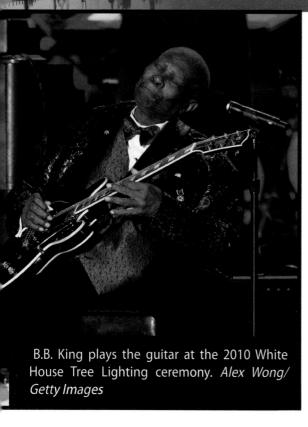

B.B. King plays the guitar at the 2010 White House Tree Lighting ceremony. *Alex Wong/ Getty Images*

continuous tours of clubs and theaters throughout the country. He often played 300 or more one-night stands a year with his 13-piece band. A long succession of hits, including "Every Day I Have the Blues," "Sweet Sixteen," and "The Thrill Is Gone," enhanced his popularity.

By the late 1960s rock guitarists acknowledged his influence, and they introduced King and his guitar, Lucille, to a wider audience. King's autobiography, *Blues All Around Me*, with David Ritz, was published in 1996.

UMM KULTHŪM

(b. 1904–d. 1975)

Umm Kulthūm was born on May 4, 1904, in Tummāy al-Zahāyrah, Egypt. Her father was a village imam who sang traditional religious songs at weddings and holidays to make ends meet. She learned to sing from him, and, when he noticed the strength of her voice, he began taking her with him. Umm Kulthūm made a name for herself singing in the towns and villages of the Egyptian delta (an area throughout which she retained a great following). By the time she was a teenager, she had become the family star.

Sometime about 1923 her family moved to Cairo, a major centre of the lucrative world of entertainment and emerging mass media production in the Middle East. There they were perceived as old-fashioned and countrified. To improve her image and acquire sophistication, Umm Kulthūm studied music and poetry from accomplished performers and scholars and copied the manners of the ladies of wealthy homes in which she was invited to sing. She soon made a name in the homes and salons of the wealthy as well as in public venues such as theatres and cabarets. By the mid-1920s she had made her first recordings and had achieved a more polished and sophisticated musical and personal style. By the end of the 1920s, she had become a sought-after performer and was one of the best-paid musicians in Cairo. Her extremely successful career in commercial recording eventually extended to radio, film, and television. In 1936 she made her first motion picture, *Wedad*, in which she played the title role. It was the first of six motion pictures in which she was to act.

By the later half of the 1930s, Kulthūm had moved from singing religious songs to performing popular tunes—often in the colloquial dialect and accompanied by a small traditional orchestra—and she became known for her emotive, passionate renditions of arrangements by the best composers, poets, and songwriters of the day. The first of these tunes, "Inta 'Umri" ("You Are My Life"), remains a modern classic. Her strong and nuanced voice and her ability to fashion multiple iterations of single lines of text drew audiences into the emotion and meaning of the poetic lyrics and extended for hours what often had been written as relatively short compositions.

Known sometimes as Kawkab al-Sharq ("Star of the East"), Umm Kulthūm had an immense repertoire, which included religious, senti-mental, and nationalistic songs. In the midst of the turmoil created by two world wars, the Great Depression of the 1930s, and the 1952 Egyptian revolution, she cultivated a public persona as a patriotic Egyptian and a devout Muslim. She sang songs in support of Egyptian independence—including "Nashid al-Jami'ah" ("The University Anthem") and "Sa'alu Qalbi" ("Ask My Heart")—and in the 1950s sang many songs in support of Egyptian leader Gamal Abdel Nasser, with whom she developed a close friendship. One of her songs associated with Nasser—"Wallahi Zaman, Ya Silahi" ("It's Been a Long Time, O Weapon of Mine")—was adopted as the Egyptian national anthem from 1960 to 1979. Her popularity was further enhanced by her generous donations to Arab causes. After Egypt's defeat in the Six-Day War of June 1967, she toured Egypt and the broader Arab world, donating the proceeds of her concerts to the Egyptian government.

Health problems plagued the singer most of her life. During the late 1940s and early '50s, she worked only on a limited basis, and on a number of occasions throughout her life she traveled to Europe and the United States for treatment of a variety of ailments. Most obviously, problems with her eyes (purportedly from years spent in front of stage lights) forced her to wear heavy sunglasses, which became a hallmark during her later life. Such was her popularity that news of her death on Feb. 3, 1975, in Cairo provoked a spontaneous outpouring of hysterical grief, and millions of admirers lined the streets for her funeral procession. She remained one of the Arab world's best-selling singers even decades after her death. In 2001 the Egyptian government established the Kawkab al-Sharq Museum in Cairo to celebrate the singer's life and accomplishments.

LEADBELLY

(b. 1885–d. 1949)

U.S. folksinger and composer Leadbelly was born Huddie William Ledbetter near Shreveport, La., probably on Jan. 21, 1885. An African American folk legend whose style influenced the hootenanny movement as well as folk music in general, he became a wandering musician who sang the blues. Although he had frequent run-ins with the law, he used his music to win a pardon and avoid work details while in jail. On a Louisiana prison farm, he was discovered in 1930 by John and Alan Lomax, who were collecting folk songs for the Library of Congress. His best-know songs, "On Top of Old Smokey" and his theme song, "Goodnight, Irene," became hits after his death in New York City on Dec. 6, 1949.

LED ZEPPELIN

The British rock band Led Zeppelin enjoyed phenomenal commercial success throughout the 1970s. Although their musical style was diverse, the band came to be best known for its influence on the development of heavy metal.

Initially called the New Yardbirds, Led Zeppelin was formed in 1968 by Jimmy Page (b. Jan. 9, 1944, in Heston, Middlesex, England), the final lead guitarist for the legendary British blues band the Yardbirds. Bassist and keyboard player John Paul Jones (b. John Baldwin on Jan. 3, 1946, in Sidcup, Kent), like Page, was a veteran studio musician; vocalist Robert Plant (b. Aug. 20, 1948, in West Bromwich, West Midlands) and drummer John Bonham (b. May 31, 1948, in Redditch, Hereford and Worcester; d. Sept. 25, 1980, in Windsor, Berkshire) came from little-known local bands. Page and Jones wrote most of the band's music, while Plant contributed lyrics and some musical ideas.

The group was influenced by various kinds of music, including early rock and roll, psychedelic rock, blues, folk, Celtic, Indian, and Arabic music. Although acoustic and folk-based music was part of the band's repertoire from its inception, it was the bottom-heavy, loud, raw, and powerful electric style that gained them their following early on. Their first two albums, *Led Zeppelin* (1968) and *Led Zeppelin II* (1969), included many of the songs that prompted the band's categorization as a precursor of heavy metal. The heaviness of songs such as "Dazed and Confused" and "Whole Lotta Love" was created by Bonham's enormous drum sound and through Page's production techniques, which emphasized drums and bass.

Plant's voice rounded out Led Zeppelin's sound. Exaggerating the vocal style of blues singers such as Howlin' Wolf and Muddy Waters, Plant created the sound that has defined much hard rock and heavy metal singing: a high range, an abundance of distortion, loud volume, and emotional excess ("Whole Lotta Love" is a classic example). Plant was, however, capable of a broader stylistic range, including tender ballads ("The Rain Song") and songs showing the influence of Indian and Arabic vocal styles ("Kashmir").

Led Zeppelin's best-known song is "Stairway to Heaven." Its gentle acoustic beginning eventually builds to an exhilarating climax featuring a lengthy electric guitar solo. This combination of acoustic and electric sections was typical for the band. The song, which was of epic length by rock standards, appeared on the band's fourth and most famous album, released untitled in 1971.

While Led Zeppelin never received the kind of critical acclaim or mainstream acceptance accorded the Beatles or the Rolling Stones, their influence on rock music has been prodigious. They are regularly cited as the originators of both hard rock and heavy metal. Their sound has been imitated by bands from Black Sabbath to Nirvana. They also inspired hard rock bands to include acoustic elements in their music and were among the first to experiment with Indian and North African music.

The group disbanded in 1980 after Bonham's alcohol-related death. The remaining members reunited in 1985 for the Live Aid benefit concert in Philadelphia and in 1988 for Atlantic Records' 40th anniversary celebration (John Bonham's son, Jason, sat in on drums). In the 1990s Page and Plant collaborated on two albums, *No Quarter* (1994) and *Walking into Clarksdale* (1998). Led Zeppelin was inducted into the Rock and Roll Hall of Fame in 1995.

FRANZ LISZT

(b. 1811–d. 1886)

The most brilliant pianist of his day, Liszt was also a distinguished composer of great originality and a major figure in the whole of Romantic music.

Franz Liszt was born on Oct. 22, 1811, in Doborján, Hungary (now Raiding, Austria). His father was employed by the Esterházy family as a steward at Doborján and was himself an amateur musician. The Esterházy family had distinguished themselves as enthusiastic patrons of music for many generations.

Liszt's father taught him to play the piano, and at the age of nine he gave concerts at Sopron and Pozsony (now Bratislava, Slovakia), as well as at Prince Nicolas Esterházy's palace. Liszt went to Vienna, where he studied with two well-known teachers, Karl Czerny and Antonio Salieri. He gave his first public concerts in Vienna in 1822 and in Paris and London in 1824. His playing moved Beethoven to kiss him. In England King George IV received him at Windsor. In Paris, where he lived for 12 years, he was sensationally successful.

In 1835 Liszt was joined in Geneva by the Countess Marie d'Agoult, though they never married. Their daughter Cosima became the wife of the conductor Hans von Bülow and then of the composer Richard Wagner. Triumphant concert tours dominated Liszt's life until September 1847, when he made his last appearance as a virtuoso.

From 1848 to 1859 he was conductor at the court and theater at Weimar. There he championed Wagner's music and produced his music dramas. Liszt also introduced and revived the works of other contemporary composers. It was his most productive period, during which he composed 12 of his symphonic poems, the *Faust* and *Dante* symphonies, the piano sonata, two piano concertos, and *Totentanz* for piano and orchestra. It was also during this period that he revised versions of the *Paganini Études* and the *Transcendental Études* for piano.

At 50 he retired to Rome. He received minor orders in the Roman Catholic Church in 1865. In Rome he was occupied with religious music, composing two oratorios and a number of smaller works. In 1869 he again began visiting Weimar regularly. The Hungarian government named him president of the Academy of Music at Budapest in 1870. Thereafter he divided his time among Rome, Weimar, and Budapest. His last works were harmonically very advanced, anticipating musical forms of the 20th century. These works were, however, long neglected. After a highly spectacular jubilee tour to Paris, London, and other cities in 1886, he died at Bayreuth, Bavaria (now in Germany), of pneumonia on July 31.

LITTLE RICHARD

(b. 1932–)

W hen rock and roll loudly introduced itself to popular culture in the 1950s, Little Richard embodied what made the music loved by some and feared by others. His voice was the loudest, his clothes were the flashiest, and his lyrics ranged from nonsense to the most sexually suggestive of the day. Along with Elvis Presley and Chuck Berry, he was on the front line of a musical revolution.

One of 12 children, Richard Wayne Penniman was born on Dec. 5, 1932, in Macon, Ga. He learned gospel music in Pentecostal churches of the Deep South, and at age 10 he started a gospel singing group, the Tiny Tots Quartet. As a teenager he left home to perform rhythm and blues in medicine shows and nightclubs, where he took the name Little Richard, achieving notoriety for high-energy onstage antics. He made his first recordings, in a soothing jump-blues style, in the early 1950s, but his breakthrough came in 1955 with the hit single "Tutti Frutti." In the year and a half that followed, he released a string of songs that sold well among both black and white audiences, including "Rip It Up," "Long Tall Sally," "Ready Teddy," "Good Golly, Miss Molly," and "Send Me Some Lovin'." Blessed with a phenomenal voice able to generate croons, wails, and screams unprecedented in popular music, Little Richard offered models of singing and musicianship that have inspired rock musicians ever since.

As his success grew, Little Richard appeared in some of the earliest rock-and-roll movies: *Don't Knock the Rock* and *The Girl Can't Help It* (both 1956) and *Mr. Rock and Roll* (1957). At the very peak of his fame, however, he concluded that rock and roll was the devil's work; he abandoned the music business, enrolled in Bible college, and became a traveling Evangelical preacher. In the mid-1960s, however, inspired by the Beatles' performances of several of his classic songs, Little Richard returned to the stage and the recording studio. Although a new song, "Bama Lama Bama Loo" (1964), invoked the fun and vitality of his heyday, record-buying youngsters were not impressed. A major recording contract in the early 1970s produced three albums—*The Rill Thing*, *King of Rock and Roll*, and *The Second Coming*—that showed Little Richard in fine voice but somewhat out of his element in the hard rock styles of the period.

In the mid-1970s Little Richard turned again to preaching before re-emerging in the entertainment industry a decade later. He began to appear at concerts and festivals and became a frequent guest on television talk shows and children's programs. In 1995 Little Richard, the self-proclaimed "architect of rock and roll," became a charter member of the Rock and Roll Hall of Fame.

MADONNA

(b. 1958–)

One of the most successful female pop performers in the United States is the singer, songwriter, actress, and entrepreneur Madonna. She was one of the first stars of music videos, performing catchy, often overtly sexual songs from her hit albums. As an actress she appeared on Broadway as well as in movies. Worldwide concert tours featuring Madonna and dancers added to her immense popularity beginning in the 1980s.

Madonna Louise Ciccone was born on Aug. 16, 1958, in Bay City, Michigan. She studied dance at the

Madonna performing on stage during one of her tours. *Kevin Mazur/WireImage/Getty Images*

University of Michigan and performed in the Alvin Ailey American Dance Theater in New York City before working in a disco revue in Paris in 1979. Upon returning to the United States, she performed with several rock groups before recording her first hit, "Holiday," in 1983. She sang about love, sex, and relationships, and her tuneful songs used dance-music beats and catchy choruses.

Madonna was the first female artist to fully exploit the potential of the music video. She worked with top designers, photographers, and directors to invent memorable sexual and satirical images. They included the knowing innocent she portrayed in "Like a Virgin" (1984), the Marilyn Monroe-like figure of "Material Girl" (1985), and the controversial red-dressed sinner who kisses a saint in "Like a Prayer" (1989). Among her other hits were "Papa Don't Preach" (1986), "Vogue" (1990), and "Justify My Love" (1990). Meanwhile she had acted in major roles in the movies *Desperately Seeking Susan* (1985), *Shanghai Surprise* (1986), and *Dick Tracy* (1990), and she appeared on Broadway in David Mamet's *Speed the Plow* (1988).

In 1991 the film *Truth or Dare* (also known as *In Bed with Madonna*), a documentary of one of her tours, appeared. By then Madonna had scored 21 top ten hits in the United States and sold some 70 million albums internationally. Committed to controlling her own career, she made a deal with Time Warner for her to run her own subsidiary recording company, named Maverick. In 1992 Madonna published *Sex*, a book featuring the singer in a variety of provocative poses. Soon afterward she temporarily withdrew from pop music to concentrate on her film career. She scored massive success in 1996 with her starring role in the film musical *Evita*.

In 1998 Madonna released her first album of new material in four years, *Ray of Light*, which was an experiment in techno music. It became a commercial and critical success, earning the singer her first Grammy Awards for her music. Her foray into electronica continued with *Music* (2000). In 2005 she returned to her dance roots with *Confessions on a Dance Floor*. *Hard Candy* (2008) was a hip-hop infused album with writing and vocal and production work by Justin Timberlake, Timbaland, and Pharrell Williams of the hit-making duo the Neptunes. With the album *MDNA* (2012), which featured cameos from women rappers M.I.A. and

Nicki Minaj, Madonna continued to prove herself a shrewd assimilator of cutting-edge musical styles. Her 2008 Sticky & Sweet Tour and 2012's MDNA Tour both broke records as the highest-grossing tours among female artists, earning Madonna numerous additional awards.

Madonna was briefly married to actor Sean Penn in the 1980s and wed English director Guy Ritchie in 2000. She and Ritchie divorced in 2008. In 2008 Madonna was inducted into the Rock and Roll Hall of Fame.

GUSTAV MAHLER

(b. 1860–d. 1911)

The great Austrian symphonist Gustav Mahler was known during his lifetime primarily as an opera and orchestra conductor. His ten symphonies and other symphony-like works are major forerunners of 20th-century musical developments, but they were rejected for the most part until the early 1960s. Largely through the efforts of his friend and disciple, the conductor Bruno Walter, his works are now performed widely and their significance recognized.

The second of 12 children, Gustav Mahler was born on July 7, 1860, in Kalischt, in what is now the Czech Republic. Showing early musical talent, he entered the Vienna Conservatory in 1875. When he failed to win the conservatory's Beethoven prize for his first significant composition, *Das klagende Lied* ("The Song of Complaint"), he turned to conducting for a more secure livelihood.

Although he was a major opera conductor, his compositions are all symphonic—even his considerable number of songs. The premiere in 1910 of his *Symphony No. 8*, known as the "Symphony of a Thousand," was the first unqualified success Mahler had ever enjoyed. He never heard his last three works—*Das Lied von der Erde* ("The Song of the Earth"), a six-movement "song-cycle symphony" for contralto and tenor soloists and orchestra, and the last two symphonies, the final one left incomplete. He brought the romantic era to a culmination with an expansive emotional expression and a grand design of structure.

As a conductor Mahler worked his way through appointments in Austria, Hungary, and Germany until he became artistic director of the Vienna Court Opera in 1897. He was a tireless taskmaster, and he achieved the highest artistic results. But he lacked tact and ran roughshod over anyone in his way. After ten years in the post, he left and was soon the principal conductor of the Metropolitan Opera in New York City. In 1909 he became conductor of the New York Philharmonic Orchestra, and again his autocratic ways forced his departure. He left in 1911, a spiritually broken man. He died a few months later in Vienna on May 18.

BOB MARLEY

(b. 1945–d. 1981)

With his band the Wailers, Jamaican singer and composer Bob Marley introduced reggae music to a worldwide audience. His thoughtful, ongoing distillation of early ska, rock steady, and reggae forms blossomed in the 1970s into an electrifying rock-influenced hybrid that made him an international superstar.

Robert Nesta Marley was born on Feb. 6, 1945, in Nine Miles, St. Ann, Jamaica. The son of a white rural overseer, Norval Sinclair Marley, and the black daughter of a local *custos* (respected backwoods squire), the former Cedella Malcolm, Bob Marley would forever remain the unique product of parallel worlds—his poetic worldview was shaped by the countryside, his music by the tough West Kingston ghetto streets. As a child Marley was known for his shy aloofness, his startling stare, and his penchant for palm reading.

By his early teens Marley was living in a government-subsidized tenement in Trench Town, a desperately poor slum of West Kingston that was often compared to an open sewer. In the early 1960s, while a schoolboy serving an apprenticeship as a welder (along with fellow aspiring singer Desmond Dekker), Marley was exposed to ska, a Jamaican amalgam of American rhythm and blues and native mento (folk-calypso) strains then catching on commercially. Marley was a fan of Fats Domino, the Moonglows, and pop singer Ricky Nelson,

Bob Marley singing live on stage. *Vincent McEvoy/Redferns/Getty Images*

but, when his big chance came in 1961 to record with producer Leslie Kong, he cut "Judge Not," a peppy ballad he had written based on rural maxims learned from his grandfather. Among his other early tracks was "One Cup of Coffee," a rendition of a 1961 hit by Texas country crooner Claude Gray.

Marley also formed a vocal group in Trench Town with friends who would later be known as Peter Tosh (byname of Winston Hubert McIntosh) and Bunny Wailer (byname of Neville O'Reilly Livingston). The trio named itself the Wailers (because, as Marley stated, "We started out crying"). Later they were joined by vocalist Junior Braithwaite and backup singers Beverly Kelso and Cherry Green.

In December 1963 the Wailers cut "Simmer Down," a song by Marley that he had used to win a talent contest in Kingston. Unlike the playful mento music that drifted from the porches of local tourist hotels or the pop and rhythm and blues filtering into Jamaica from American radio stations, "Simmer Down" was an urgent anthem from the shantytown precincts of the Kingston underclass. A huge overnight smash, it played an important role in recasting the agenda for stardom in Jamaican music circles. No longer did one have to parrot the stylings of overseas entertainers; it was possible to write raw, uncompromising songs for and about the disenfranchised people of the West Indian slums.

This bold stance transformed both Marley and his island nation, engendering the urban poor with a pride that would become a pronounced source of identity (and a catalyst for class-related tension) in Jamaican culture—as would the Wailers' Rastafarian faith, a creed popular among the impoverished people of the Caribbean. The Wailers did well in Jamaica during the mid-1960s with their ska records, and reggae material created in 1969–71 with producer Lee Perry increased their stature. Once they released *Catch a Fire* in the early 1970s (the first reggae album conceived as more than a mere singles compilation), their uniquely rock-contoured reggae gained a global audience. It also earned the charismatic Marley superstar status, which gradually led to the dissolution of the original trio in about 1974.

Despite the dissolution of the original group, Marley continued to guide the Wailers band through a series of potent, topical albums. By this point Marley also was backed by a trio of female vocalists that included his wife, Rita; she, like many of Marley's children, later experienced her own recording success. Featuring eloquent songs like "No Woman, No Cry," "Exodus," "Could You Be Loved," "Coming in from the Cold," "Jamming," and "Redemption Song," Bob Marley's landmark albums included *Natty Dread* (1974), *Live!* (1975), *Rastaman Vibration* (1976), *Exodus* (1977), *Kaya* (1978), *Uprising* (1980), and the posthumous *Confrontation* (1983).

Marley also loomed large as a political figure and in 1976 survived what was believed to have been a politically motivated assassination attempt. His attempt to broker a truce between Jamaica's warring political factions led in April 1978 to his headlining the One Love Peace Concert. In April 1981, the Jamaican government awarded Marley the Order of Merit. He died of cancer a month later, on May 11, 1981, in Miami, Fla.

Although his songs had been some of the best-liked and most critically acclaimed music in the popular canon, Marley was far more renowned in death than he had been in life. *Legend* (1984), a retrospective of his work, became the best-selling reggae album ever, with international sales of more than 12 million copies.

FELIX MENDELSSOHN

(b. 1809–d. 1847)

The composer, pianist, and conductor Felix Mendelssohn was a pivotal figure of 19th-century romanticism. He was also a major force in the revival of the music of Johann Sebastian Bach.

Jakob Ludwig Felix Mendelssohn-Bartholdy was born in Hamburg, Germany, on Feb. 3, 1809, a grandson of the philosopher Moses Mendelssohn. During his boyhood young Mendelssohn wrote many compositions, and he appeared as a pianist in 1818. By 1827 he had composed an overture to *A Midsummer Night's Dream*, his first mature work.

Mendelssohn conducted Bach's *St. Matthew Passion* in Berlin in 1829, an event that marked a revival in the performance of Bach's vocal music. That year he was in London, where he conducted his *Symphony in C Minor*, and a visit to Scotland inspired the *Hebrides Overture*. This was the first of ten trips to Great Britain, where he established his main reputation and became a favorite of Queen Victoria.

Mendelssohn's output was considerable, especially considering his short lifetime. Works include the *Scottish*, *Italian*, and *Reformation* symphonies; two piano concerti and one for violin; the oratorios *St. Paul* and *Elijah* (*Hymn of Praise* is considered a symphony-cantata); chamber music; piano music, including *48 Songs Without Words*; many songs; and organ pieces.

In 1833 Mendelssohn became music director in Düsseldorf, Germany, where he introduced the masses of Beethoven and Cherubini and the cantatas of Bach. Two years later he was appointed conductor of the Gewandhaus Orchestra in Leipzig, soon making it the most prestigious symphonic organization in Germany. In 1843 he founded the

TOP 101 MUSICIANS

Leipzig Conservatory, where he and Robert Schumann taught composition. After the sudden death of his sister Fanny in May 1847, Mendelssohn's health rapidly deteriorated, and he died in Leipzig on November 4.

JONI MITCHELL

(b. 1943–)

As one of the most talented and unique female performers in rock, Canadian singer, songwriter, and guitarist Joni Mitchell enjoyed a long and varied career beginning in the 1960s. Over the years her popularity soared and waned. A huge commercial success early in her career, she became relatively anonymous by the mid-1980s but regained her star status in the 1990s with several well-received albums. Considered one of the greatest female acoustic guitarists in recent music history, Mitchell survived personal and professional disappointment that inspired folk-pop confessionals and moody, jazz-tinged ballads.

Joni Mitchell was born Roberta Joan Anderson on Nov. 7, 1943, in Fort Macleod, Alberta, Canada, to William Anderson, a grocery store manager, and his wife, Myrtle, a teacher. An only child, Joni was raised in an isolated, remote area. Throughout her childhood Joni had many illnesses, including polio, which she contracted at age nine. After a difficult recovery she attended high school, where her average academic performance paled in comparison to her passion for music and art. Upon graduation she enrolled at the Alberta College of Art but stayed only a year before heading east to Toronto, where she began playing the local folk circuit. At 20 years old, Mitchell found herself unmarried and pregnant. She married an older folksinger, Chuck Mitchell (not the child's father), and she moved with him to Detroit, Mich. The marriage fell apart within a few years. Unable to care for her child, Mitchell gave her daughter up for adoption and moved to Manhattan, where she became involved in the New York music scene.

With the help of Byrds vocalist David Crosby, Mitchell landed her first record contract with Reprise Records. Her debut album, *Joni Mitchell* (1968), sold well and was followed by a series of successful albums: *Clouds* (1969); *Ladies of the Canyon* (1970), which included her first charted single, "Big Yellow Taxi"; *Blue* (1971); *For the Roses* (1972); *Court and Spark* (1974), which featured "Free Man in Paris" and "Help Me"; and *Hejira* (1976).

Mitchell's songs dealt with her own emotional struggles and romantic liaisons (including those with well-known musicians Jackson Browne, James Taylor, and Graham Nash). Yet, as she explored other musical styles, her popularity declined. Her bold collaboration with jazz great Charles Mingus on *Mingus* (1979) had a mixed reception. Mitchell's overtly romantic, poetic songs were out of step with the prevailing punk aesthetic of the day. After she married musician-producer Larry Klein in 1982 and released several albums that were basically ignored, Mitchell spent much of her time indulging her passion for painting. In addition to creating the art for each of her album covers, Mitchell also exhibited her art around the world.

During the 1990s Mitchell went through another cycle of personal and professional change. She and Klein divorced in 1982. Her health deteriorated as she began suffering from postpolio syndrome. In 1991 Mitchell released *Night Ride Home*, followed several years later by the critically acclaimed *Turbulent Indigo* (1994), which earned her several Grammy Awards and thrust her into the spotlight again. In 1995 Mitchell received Billboard magazine's Century Award. She subsequently released *Hits* and *Misses* (both 1996). Joni Mitchell was inducted into the Rock and Roll Hall of Fame in 1997.

BILL MONROE

(b. 1911–d. 1996)

U.S. singer, songwriter, and musician Bill Monroe influenced generations of country and rock musicians. He developed the uniquely American blend of blues, gospel, jazz, country, and even Celtic folk that characterizes bluegrass music; he was widely recognized as the father of bluegrass. In a career spanning six decades, Monroe sold more than 50 million records. He received numerous accolades in his career, including a 1986 United States Senate resolution recognizing his contributions to American culture. In 1997 he was inducted into the Rock and Roll Hall of Fame in the category of early influences.

William Smith Monroe was born on Sept. 13, 1911, in rural Rosine, Ky., the youngest of eight children. He was raised in a musical family; his mother sang and played several instruments, and his uncle was a fiddler. At age nine, Bill took up the mandolin because his older siblings already played the fiddle and guitar. Bill left home at 18, moving to East Chicago, Ind., where he worked with his older brothers in an oil refinery. Within a few years he and his brothers had begun playing in small venues in the Midwest, eventually moving to North Carolina, where they became a popular local blues act.

By 1936 Monroe and his brother were recording for RCA Records. After a few years, however, the Monroe Brothers split up their act and Monroe formed his own group, the Kentuckians. Later, the band became the Blue Grass Boys, named after Monroe's beloved Kentucky, the Bluegrass State. The Blue Grass Boys joined the Grand Ole Opry in 1939 and subsequently toured with the Opry road show. Monroe's band attracted a variety of performers. Over the years more than 100 different musicians played with his ensemble.

In the mid-1940s Monroe put together his most talented group of musicians: vocalist and guitarist Lester Flatt, banjo player Earl Scruggs, fiddler Chubby Wise, and bass player Howard Watts. Combining high vocal harmonies with the solid bluegrass sounds of mandolin, fiddle, rhythm guitar, and bass, the quintet recorded such classic country and western hits as "Kentucky Waltz" (1946), "Footprints in the Snow" (1946), "Blue Moon of Kentucky" (1947), which later became a hit for Elvis Presley, and "Wicked Path of Sin" (1948). From 1946 until 1959 Monroe and his band had nine top 30 country hits.

After Scruggs and Flatt left to go out on their own, Monroe found replacements and throughout the 1950s turned out what some consider his greatest body of work, including "My Little Georgia Rose," "I'm Blue, I'm Lonesome," "Uncle Pen," "The First Whippoorwill," "Roanoke," "Sitting Alone in the Moonlight," and "On and On."

Although the makeup of his bands changed and evolved, Monroe continued recording into the 1980s. He was elected into the Country Music Hall of Fame in 1970, featured on the *Stars of the Bluegrass Hall of*

Fame (1986) album, and earned the first Grammy awarded for bluegrass music for his album *Southern Favor* (1988).

Monroe was awarded the Academy of Recording Arts and Sciences lifetime achievement award in 1993. Still performing in his 80s, Monroe released several albums in the 1990s, including a four-CD retrospective, *The Music of Bill Monroe* (1994). He was also featured in film documentaries depicting the history of bluegrass music. He died on Sept. 9, 1996, in Nashville, Tenn.

WOLFGANG AMADEUS MOZART

(b. 1756–d. 1791)

A central figure of the Viennese classical school, Mozart is often considered the greatest musical genius of all time. His output—especially in view of his short life—was enormous, including 16 operas, 41 symphonies, 27 piano and 5 violin concerti, 25 string quartets, 19 masses, and other works in every form popular in his time. Perhaps his greatest single achievement is in the characterization of his operatic figures.

Wolfgang Amadeus Mozart was born on Jan. 27, 1756, in Salzburg, Austria, the son of Leopold Mozart, composer to the archbishop and a well-known violinist and author of a celebrated theoretical treatise. From 1762 he took young Mozart and his older sister, Maria Anna (called Nannerl), on tours throughout Europe in which they performed as harpsichordists and pianists—both separately and together. They gave public concerts, played at the various courts, and met the leading musicians of the day. The child prodigy also performed as a violinist and organist and received numerous commissions. His first published works were four violin sonatas, which he composed in Paris in 1764. In London he came under the influence of Johann Christian Bach. In 1768 young Mozart became honorary concertmaster for the archbishop.

On the first Italian tour, from 1769 to 1771, Mozart studied counterpoint with Giovanni Battista Martini, and in 1773 he came under the influence of the music of Franz Joseph Haydn in Vienna. A new archbishop had been installed in 1772, ending what had been

Wolfgang Amadeus Mozart. *Sean Gallup/ Getty Images*

a cordial relationship between employer and employee. By 1777 the situation had become so strained that the young composer asked to be relieved of his duties, and the archbishop grudgingly gave his permission.

Mozart went with his mother in 1777 to Munich and Mannheim, Germany, and to Paris, where she died. This trip produced seven violin sonatas, seven piano sonatas, a ballet, and three symphonic works, including *Sinfonie D-Dur KV 297* (commonly known in English as the *Paris Symphony*). Back in Salzburg in 1779, Mozart composed the *Krönungsmesse* (*Coronation Mass*), *Missa solemnis*, two symphonies, the *Posthorn* serenade, and the opera seria *Idomeneo*, his first mature stage work.

When the final break between Mozart and the archbishop came in 1781, the musician had been seeking a position for some time but without success. It was not until 1787 that Emperor Joseph II finally engaged him as chamber composer—and then at a salary greatly reduced from that of his predecessor, Christoph Willibald Gluck. Mozart's financial situation became steadily worse, and he was forced to incur ever-increasing debts that hung over him until his death.

In the meantime his opera *Die Entführung aus dem Serail* (*The Abduction from the Seraglio*) was a great success in 1782; in the same year he married Constanze Weber, the daughter of friends. He composed his *Große Messe in c-Moll* (*Great Mass in C minor*) for her, and she was soprano soloist in its premiere.

During the last ten years of his life, Mozart produced most of his great piano concerti; the four horn concerti; the *Haffner*, *Prague*, *Linz*, and *Jupiter* symphonies; the six string quartets dedicated to Haydn; five string quintets; and the major operas *Le nozze di Figaro* (*The Marriage of Figaro*), *Don Giovanni*, *Così fan tutte* (*Thus Do They All*), *La clemenza di Tito* (*The Clemency of Titus*), and *Die Zauberflöte* (*The Magic Flute*). Mozart was unable to complete his final work, the *Requiem*, because of illness. He died in Vienna on Dec. 5, 1791, and was buried in a mass grave. Although the exact nature of his illness is unknown, there is no evidence that Mozart's death was caused deliberately.

MUDDY WATERS

(b. 1915–d. 1983)

A master of the vibrant "Chicago sound," Muddy Waters was a dynamic blues guitarist and singer who played a significant role in creating the modern ensemble blues style. He was a major influence on a wide range of musical styles, from rock and roll and rhythm and blues, to soul and funk. Along the way, he helped to shape the stylings of musicians such as Jimi Hendrix, Eric Clapton, Bob Dylan, Chuck Berry, Bonnie Raitt, and the Rolling Stones.

McKinley Morganfield was born on Apr. 4, 1915, in Rolling Fork, Miss., where his parents were sharecroppers on a plantation. When Morganfield was three his mother passed away, and the boy was sent to live with his maternal grandmother, who lived and worked at Stovall's Plantation in Clarksdale. Growing up amid the harsh poverty of the Mississippi Delta region, the young man was drawn to the power and drama of the region's music and storytelling traditions. At 13, while working as a farmhand, he taught himself to play the harmonica; four years later, he took up the guitar. He was especially influenced by the classic Delta blues fingerpicking and bottleneck slide guitar styles of Robert Johnson and Son House, and he practiced endlessly to emulate these. Within a year, Morganfield had mastered the instrument and developed a style of his own. Soon he was playing at local clubs and "juke joints" around the Delta, billing himself as "Muddy Waters," a nickname he had acquired as a child. During this period, however, he continued to work on local plantations.

Waters was first recorded in 1941 for the United States Library of Congress by archivist Alan Lomax. In 1943 Waters moved to Chicago, where he began playing in clubs and bars on the south and west sides. However, the noisy clubs made it difficult for audiences to hear Waters's acoustic guitar. Like many other players, he found that amplifying the instrument was necessary if he wanted to be heard. What he had not realized, however, was that using an amplifier changed the tone of the guitar. Waters readily adapted his rural Delta blues and bottleneck styles, and the urban electric sound of Chicago blues was born. His electrically amplified band, including pianist Otis Spann and harmonica virtuoso Little Walter, created integral support for Waters's passionate singing, which featured dramatic shouts, swoops, and falsetto moans. His repertoire of songs, much of which he composed, included the mournful "Blow Wind Blow" and "Trouble No More" and the boastful and teasing "Got My Mojo Working" and "I'm Your Hoochie Coochie Man," as well as the highly sensual "Rock Me."

Waters's sound captured the attention of Phil and Leonard Chess, two brothers who had founded a recording company in Chicago. Waters made his first recording for the brothers, on their Aristocrat Records label, in 1947. He continued to record for them on their new label, Chess Records, throughout the 1950s, and he was considered the foremost advocate of modern Chicago blues. During this period he worked with many of the greatest names in blues, including Willie Dixon and a young man he had personally mentored, Buddy Guy.

Waters toured clubs in the South and Midwest in the 1940s and '50s. After 1958, Waters played concert tours around the United States and Europe, including frequent performances at jazz, folk, and blues festivals. In later years he concentrated more on singing and less on playing guitar, but he continued to serve as mentor to a new generation of blues-influenced rock musicians. He died on Apr. 30, 1983, in Westmont, Ill. In 1987 Waters was inducted into the Rock and Roll Hall of Fame in Cleveland, Ohio.

NIRVANA

U.S. alternative rock group Nirvana were the leaders in the musical style called grunge. Their breakthrough album, *Nevermind* (1991), gave voice to the post–baby boom young adults known as Generation X. The members were Kurt Cobain (b. Feb. 20, 1967, Aberdeen, Wash.–d. Apr. 5, 1994, Seattle, Wash.), Krist Novoselic (b. May 16, 1965, Compton, Calif.), and Dave Grohl (b. Jan. 14, 1969, Warren, Ohio).

Nirvana was born in Aberdeen as part of the post-punk underground scene that centered in Olympia, Wash., but they recorded their first single, "Love Buzz," and album, *Bleach*, for an independent record

Nirvana performing on *MTV Live* and *Loud. Jeff Kravitz/FilmMagic, Inc./Getty Images*

company in Seattle. They refined this mix of 1960s-style pop and 1970s heavy metal hard rock on *Nevermind*, their first album for a major label. *Nevermind*, featuring the hit "Smells Like Teen Spirit," was the first full expression of punk concerns to achieve mass market success in the United States.

Nirvana used extreme changes of tempo and volume to express anger and alienation: a quiet, tuneful verse switched into a ferocious, distorted chorus. In the fashion of many 1970s punk groups, guitarist-singer-songwriter Cobain set powerful rock against sarcastic, allusive lyrics that explored hopelessness and surrender. Influenced by the punk ethic that to succeed was to fail, Nirvana abhorred the media onslaught that accompanied their rapid rise to fame. Success brought celebrity, and Cobain, typecast as a self-destructive rock star, courted controversy both with his advocacy of feminism and gay rights and with his embroilment in a sequence of drug- and gun-related escapades—a number of which involved his wife, Courtney Love, leader of the band Hole.

Like *Nevermind*, the band's third album, *In Utero* (1993), reached number one on the U.S. album charts. By this point, however, Cobain's heroin use was out of control. After a reputed suicide attempt in Rome, Italy, in March 1994, he entered a Los Angeles, Calif., treatment center. In a mysterious sequence of events, he returned to Seattle, where he shot and killed himself in his lakeside home. Subsequent concert releases, notably *Unplugged in New York* (1994) and *From the Muddy Banks of the Wishkah* (1996), only added to Nirvana's legend. In 2002 the greatest-hits album *Nirvana* appeared and included the previously unreleased single "You Know You're Right." That year a collection of Cobain's journals was also published.

CHARLIE PARKER

(b. 1920–d. 1955)

The legendary jazzman known as Bird had a profound influence on an entire generation of jazz performers, and musicians still pay tribute to his innovative bop style. After the death of Charlie Parker, hipsters wrote "BIRD LIVES" graffiti on city sidewalks and walls. The celebrated nickname is short for Yardbird—a reference to his appetite for fried chicken or, according to other sources, his habit of hanging out in the alleys behind jazz clubs to play his alto saxophone when he was too young and inept to be allowed inside.

Charles Parker, Jr., was born on Aug. 29, 1920, in Kansas City, Kan. In 1927 his family moved to Kansas City, Mo., which was the center of a blues-based style of jazz. He played the tuba in the high school band, but his mother thought it looked funny and bought him an alto saxophone. Because he taught himself how to play it, he used all 12 keys and developed great facility. By the age of 16, he had a wife and child and was earning $1.25 a night as a musician.

Bird has been credited with inventing the harmonic changes that bop brought to jazz. He claimed that he had become bored with playing the same arrangements night after night. Soon after he moved to New York City in 1939, Bird found the changes when he started playing the upper parts of the chords.

Bird's remarkable gifts as an improviser at after-hours clubs brought him an offer to participate in jam sessions at Minton's Playhouse in Harlem in late 1941. He developed the shape of bop with such artists as Thelonious Monk and Dizzy Gillespie. Beginning in 1945, Bird made many recordings, including his first with Dizzy and his first with Miles Davis on trumpet. As a result of drug addiction, he broke down while recording "Lover Man" in Los Angeles in July 1946 and was confined to Camarillo State Hospital.

Parker described his music simply as "playing clean and looking for the pretty notes." He often created new pieces based on the harmonies of popular songs. Such works as "Anthropology," written with Gillespie and based on George Gershwin's "I Got Rhythm," became jazz standards. Some of his most popular songs are "Parker's Mood," "Confirmation," "Ornithology," "Billie's Bounce," and "Now's the Time."

In 1949–51 Parker made three trips to Europe. He was admitted to Bellevue Hospital in New York City in September 1954 after a suicide attempt. His last public appearance was at Birdland, a club in New York City named for him. He died in New York City on March 12, 1955.

PARLIAMENT-FUNKADELIC

Led by raucous, flamboyant lead singer George Clinton (b. July 22, 1940, in Kannapolis, N.C.), the loose collective of musicians that made up the bands Parliament and Funkadelic (as well as various offshoots) created some of black pop music's most outrageous and successful dance music of the 1970s. Combining funk rhythms, psychedelic guitar, and group harmonies with jazzed-up horns, Clinton and his ever-evolving bands set the tone for many post-disco and post-punk groups of the 1980s and 1990s. With his flair for showmanship—early concerts had Clinton jumping out of a coffin onstage and his band running around in diapers—Clinton and his entourage performed some of the lengthiest, most improvisational live shows of any group besides the Grateful Dead.

As a teenager in Plainfield, N.J., in the mid-1950s, George Clinton was working at a barbershop when he founded the Parliaments, a doo-wop style group. The group had marginal success when Clinton moved to Detroit in the 1960s, where he became a staff writer for Motown Records. The Parliaments finally landed their first hit with the single "(I Wanna) Testify" (1967), a love song written by Clinton. When a legal battle arose over use of the group's name, Clinton and the singers from the Parliaments began recording with their backup band under the name Funkadelic for Westbound Records. Even after the lawsuit was settled, Clinton continued to record with his band separately under both names (though he dropped the "s" from Parliaments). Later, the band's personnel would use various names, such as P-Funk, the offshoot Bootsy's Rubber Band, and the P-Funk All Stars.

During the 1970s Clinton's group included R&B musicians from other bands, including James Brown bassist William "Bootsy" Collins and Ohio Players guitarist Eddie Hazel and keyboardist Bernie Worrell. With a series of hits on both the pop and R&B charts—"Flash Light" (1978), "Aqua Boogie" (1978), and "One Nation Under a Groove" (1978) all became number one R&B hits—Parliament-Funkadelic challenged Earth, Wind & Fire as the top black band of the decade. In the 1980s, however, the diversity and size of Parliament-Funkadelic seemed to contribute to its demise. Clinton released a solo album under his own name—*Computer Games* (1982), which included the number one hit single "Atomic Dog"—and when several members left to record on their own the band lost its core. In addition, the Parliament-Funkadelic sound was popping up in mainstream funk and hip-hop. Clinton took some time off from performing and recording to produce and write. He resurfaced in the late 1980s with *The Cinderella Theory* (1989) and reassembled Parliament-Funkadelic for concerts.

In 1993, Parliament-Funkadelic performed at President Bill Clinton's Youth Inaugural Ball. With guest rappers Ice Cube and Yo-Yo, Clinton released *Hey Man...* (1993), which did not fare well commercially, though it revitalized Clinton and Parliament-Funkadelic's public image enough to land them a spot on the 1994 Lollapalooza tour. Parliament-Funkadelic was inducted into the Rock and Roll Hall of Fame in 1997.

LUCIANO PAVAROTTI

(b. 1935–d. 2007)

Italian opera singer Luciano Pavarotti was considered by many critics as the greatest lyric tenor of his time. Even in the highest register, his voice was noted for its purity of tone. In addition to singing in opera houses, Pavarotti recorded extensively and achieved commercial popularity through his televised opera performances.

Pavarotti was born on Oct. 12, 1935, in Modena, Italy. He graduated from a teaching institute there in 1955 and then taught elementary school for two years. He studied opera privately, mostly in Mantua. After winning the Concorso Internazionale, a singing competition, he made his professional operatic debut in 1961 in Reggio Emilia, Italy, as Rodolfo in Giacomo Puccini's *La bohème*. He then played in opera houses throughout Europe and Australia. In 1968 he made his debut at New York City's Metropolitan Opera House and from 1971 was a regular performer there. His most notable operatic roles include the duke in Giuseppe Verdi's *Rigoletto*, Tonio in Gaetano Donizetti's *La fille du régiment* (*The Daughter of the Regiment*), with its demanding sequence

Luciano Pavarotti performing at a concert in Serbia. *Marko Rupena/Shutterstock.com*

of high Cs, Arturo in Vincenzo Bellini's *I puritani* (*The Puritans*), and Radamès in Verdi's *Aïda*.

Pavarotti became known to a broader public than opera connoisseurs; his concerts, recordings, and television appearances—which provided ample opportunity to display his ebullient personality— gained him a wide popular following. In 1990 he began to tour with Plácido Domingo and José Carreras as the Three Tenors, singing popular operatic arias and other songs to large audiences in arenas and sports stadiums worldwide. Pavarotti gave his final performance on the operatic stage in 2004, though he continued to sing publicly until 2006. Among his many prizes and awards were five Grammy Awards and a Kennedy Center Honor in 2001. Pavarotti died on Sept. 6, 2007, in his hometown of Modena.

EDITH PIAF

(b. 1915–d. 1963)

The French singer and actress Edith Piaf became internationally famous for her interpretation of the *chanson*, or French ballad. Her singing reflected the tragedies of her own life. Among her most famous songs was "Non, je ne regrette rien" ("No, I Don't Regret Anything").

Edith Giovanna Gassion was born on Dec. 19, 1915, in Paris, France. Her mother, a café singer, abandoned her at birth, and she was raised by her grandmother. She became blind at the age of three as a complication of meningitis but recovered her sight four years later. Her father, a circus acrobat, took her along on tours and first encouraged her to sing. She sang in the streets of Paris until she was discovered by a cabaret owner who gave her her first nightclub job and suggested that she change her name to Piaf, Parisian slang for "sparrow," in apparent reference to her small size. Her debut was acclaimed by the actor and singer Maurice Chevalier, who happened to be in the audience.

In 1935 Piaf made her theatrical debut, and within a few years she was singing in the large music halls of Paris. During World War II she would perform only for French prisoners of war and aided several in their escapes. After the war she toured Europe, South America, and the United States. Her simple yet dramatic style and throaty, tender voice with its tragic overtones brought her wide acclaim and never ceased to move her audiences. Despite her success, however, her life continued to be marred by illness, accidents, and personal unhappiness. She died on Oct. 11, 1963, in Paris.

COLE PORTER

(b. 1891–d. 1964)

U.S. composer and lyricist Cole Porter was widely successful in the field of American musicals. His large output of work reflects a sophisticated, polished musical style.

Cole Albert Porter was born on June 9, 1891, in Peru, Ind., the grandson of a millionaire speculator. He began violin study at the age of six and piano at eight. When he was 10 he composed an operetta in the style of Gilbert and Sullivan; his first composition, a waltz, was published a year later. Before graduating from Yale University with a bachelor's degree in 1913, he composed about 300 songs, including "Eli," "Bulldog," and "Bingo Eli Yale." Porter later studied at Harvard Law

School (1914) and the Harvard Graduate School of Arts and Sciences in music (1915–16). He made his Broadway debut with the musical comedy *See America First* (1916), which closed after 15 performances.

Porter wrote his first successful Broadway musical, *Fifty Million Frenchmen*, in 1929. Perhaps his greatest financial and artistic success came from *Kiss Me, Kate* in 1948. His other musical comedies included *Gay Divorce* (1932), *Anything Goes* (1934), *Jubilee* (1935), *Panama Hattie* (1940), *Can-Can* (1953), and *Silk Stockings* (1955). At the same time, Porter worked on a number of motion pictures. Among his hundreds of songs were "Night and Day," "You're the Top," "Begin the Beguine," "I've Got You Under My Skin," "In the Still of the Night," "Love for Sale," and "It's Delovely." Porter died on Oct. 15, 1964, in Santa Monica, Calif.

ELVIS PRESLEY

(b. 1935–d. 1977)

One of the most successful entertainers ever, Elvis Presley dominated popular music in the United States from the release of his first big record, "Heartbreak Hotel," in 1956. His records, 45 of which sold more than a million copies each, his 33 motion pictures, and his appearances on television and in live concerts made the young singer into a one-man industry who by the mid-1960s was the highest-paid performer in show business history. His death in 1977 in no way diminished his popularity with his fans. His records continued to sell, and his legend brought on a whole generation of imitators.

Elvis Aaron Presley was born on Jan. 8, 1935, in Tupelo, Miss. In 1949 the family moved to Memphis, Tenn., where young Presley attended L.C. Humes High School, graduating in 1953. That summer he came to the attention of Sam Phillips, president of Sun Records, when he went there to make a personal recording intended as a present for his mother. Presley made his first commercial recording for Sun the following year, and Colonel Tom Parker, who managed his career from that time, arranged for him to make a series of personal appearances.

In 1955 RCA Victor bought his recording contract from Phillips, and by 1956 Presley was a best-selling recording artist and television

Fans reach out for Elvis as he performs. *Hulton Archive/Getty Images*

star. His hip gyrations, which some viewers thought too suggestive, earned him the nickname Elvis the Pelvis. *Love Me Tender*, his first film, was released that same year.

Drafted into the Army in 1958, Presley went through regular training and then served as a truck driver in West Germany until his discharge in 1960. Resuming his career under Parker's supervision, he worked up a touring act, based in Las Vegas, Nev., and attracted an ever-expanding public. He bought Graceland, his lavish Memphis mansion, using it as a retreat from the enthusiasm of his public. In 1967 he married Priscilla Beaulieu. The couple, who had a daughter the following year, were divorced in 1973.

Unable to go anywhere without being mobbed by fans, Presley became increasingly reclusive. He gained weight and took various prescription drugs. He died of heart failure in Memphis on Aug. 16, 1977.

PRINCE

(b. 1958–)

U.S. musician Prince was born on June 7, 1958, in Minneapolis, Minn. Prince Rogers Nelson was named after the Prince Rogers Trio, a jazz group led by his father. Prince was playing in a band by the age of 12 and at 17 broke into the music business. He released his first album in 1978; by the 1980s he was a star, with such hit albums as *1999* (1982), which went platinum; *Purple Rain* (1984), the sound track to his widely praised motion picture; and *Batman* (1989), the sound track to the 1989 film *Batman*. His often sexually explicit lyrics and stage performances made him a controversial figure. In 1993 he changed his name to a symbol he designed that combined the symbols for "male" (♀) and "female" (♂), which he later came to dub the Love Symbol. Lacking a pronounceable name, he was popularly referred to as "The Artist Formerly Known as Prince" or simply "The Artist."

Prince subsequently underwent a highly publicized struggle with Warner Bros. Records, pointing to its refusal to release his new material in rapid succession as creative limitation. The record label cited fears of market saturation, and Prince swiftly released new material as a means of fulfilling his contractual obligations and terminating his agreement with Warner Bros. In 1996, he had fulfilled his contract with the record label and released an album *Emancipation* on his own independent label. In 1998, he signed with Arista Records and in 2000, he resumed using the stage name "Prince." He continued releasing new material and touring, including the albums *LOtUSFLOW3R* (2009) and 20Ten (2010). In 2004, he was inducted into the Rock and Roll Hall of Fame.

PUBLIC ENEMY

Public Enemy is an American rap group whose dense, layered sound and radical political message made them among the most popular, controversial, and influential hip-hop artists of the late 1980s and early 1990s. The original members were Chuck D (byname of Carlton Ridenhour; b. Aug. 1, 1960, Queens, New York), Flavor Flav (byname of William Drayton; b. March 16, 1959, Long Island, New York), Terminator X (byname of Norman Lee Rogers; b. Aug. 25, 1966, New York City), and Professor Griff (byname of Richard Griffin; b. Aug. 1, 1960, Long Island).

Public Enemy was formed in 1982 at Adelphi University on Long Island, New York, by a group of young, black rappers who came primarily from the suburbs. Chuck D, Hank Shocklee, Bill Stephney, and Flavor Flav collaborated on a program on college radio. Reputedly, Def Jam producer Rick Rubin was so taken with Chuck D's booming voice that he begged him to record. Public Enemy resulted and brought radical black political ideology to pop music in an unprecedented fashion on albums with titles that read like party invitations for leftists and warning stickers for the right wing: *Yo! Bum Rush the Show* (1987), *It Takes a Nation of Millions to Hold Us Back* (1988), *Fear of a Black Planet* (1990), and *Apocalypse 91... The Enemy Strikes Black* (1991).

Acclaimed as Public Enemy's masterpiece, *It Takes a Nation of Millions to Hold Us Back* revived the messages of the Black Panther Party and Malcolm X. On tracks such as "Night of the Living Baseheads," "Black Steel in the Hour of Chaos," and "Don't Believe the Hype," the strident, eloquent lyrics of Chuck D combined with bombastic, dissonant, and poignantly detailed backing tracks created by Public Enemy's production team, the Bomb Squad (Shocklee, his brother Keith, Chuck D, and Eric "Vietnam" Adler), to produce songs challenging the status quo in both hip-hop and racial politics. The Bomb Squad sampled (composed with other recordings) a wide variety of genres and sounds, including classic funk tracks by James Brown, jazz, the thrash-metal of Anthrax, sirens, and agitprop speeches. Flavor Flav provided a comic foil for Chuck D.

Comments by Professor Griff to the *Washington Times* in 1989 brought charges of anti-Semitism, which ultimately resulted in his leaving the group. Public Enemy's open admiration for the Nation of Islam leader Louis Farrakhan also brought it into conflict with Jewish organizations. While Public Enemy's activism inspired other artists to take up topical themes, the group's influence waned in the early 1990s as younger performers associated with gangsta rap such as N.W.A. and Snoop Doggy Dogg came to the fore. The group seemed to have folded after *Muse Sick-n-Hour Mess Age* (1994), but in 1998 they produced a new album of songs for Spike Lee's film *He Got Game* and went on tour.

Breaking ties with Def Jam, Public Enemy went on to release music on various independent record labels into the 21st century, but the recordings failed to attract much attention. In 2013 the group was inducted into the Rock and Roll Hall of Fame.

GIACOMO PUCCINI

(b. 1858–d. 1924)

After Giuseppe Verdi, Giacomo Puccini is considered the greatest Italian opera composer. He is noted for such enduringly popular works as *Madama Butterfly* (*Madame Butterfly*) and *La bohème*.

Giacomo Antonio Domenico Michele Secondo Maria Puccini was born on Dec. 22, 1858, in Lucca, Tuscany. The heads of his family for four generations had been professional musicians. He was five years old when his father died. His mother chose the fifth born of her seven children to carry on the Puccini musical tradition. Young Puccini studied at the Pacini Institute of Music in Lucca. At first he was an indifferent student. Then, encouraged by a sympathetic teacher, he began to show promise as a composer and as a church organist. At about 17, inspired by a performance of Verdi's *Aïda*, he determined to specialize in composing for the operatic stage.

Aided by a grant from the queen of Italy, he was able to pursue this goal in Milan, the operatic center. He attended the Milan Conservatory from 1880 to 1883. His first opera, *Le villi* ("The Fairies"), was produced in 1884; his second, *Edgar*, in 1889. During the next 15 years were premieres of four well-known works: *Manon Lescaut* (1893), *La bohème* (1896), *Tosca* (1900), and *Madama Butterfly* (1904). In 1907 Puccini visited New York City to attend the first Metropolitan Opera production of *Madama Butterfly*. There he conceived the idea of writing an opera with an American setting. The result was *La fanciulla del West* (*The Girl of the West*) (1910).

In all Puccini composed 12 operas. The final one, *Turandot*, was unfinished. Puccini died on Nov. 29, 1924, in Brussels, Belgium. *Turandot* was first performed at La Scala in Milan on Apr. 26, 1926. Its last two scenes were completed by Franco Alfano after Puccini's death.

TITO PUENTE

(b. 1923–d. 2000)

Tito Puente was one of the leading figures in Latin jazz. His bravura showmanship and string of mambo dance hits in the 1950s earned him the nickname "King of Mambo."

The son of Puerto Rican immigrants, Puente was born on Apr. 20, 1923, New York, New York, and grew up in New York City's Spanish Harlem. He became a professional musician at age 13. He later studied at the Juilliard School and eventually learned to play a number of instruments, including the piano, saxophone, vibraphone, and timbales (paired high-pitched drums). After an apprenticeship in the historic Machito Orchestra (a New York-based Latin jazz group established in 1939), he served in the navy during World War II.

Tito Puente playing the timbales live. *Frank Micelotta/Hulton Archive/Getty Images*

In 1947 Puente formed his own 10-piece band, which he expanded two years later to include four trumpets, three trombones, and four saxophones, as well as a number of percussionists and vocalists. With other Latin musicians such as Tito Rodríguez and Pérez Prado, he helped give rise in the 1950s to the golden age of mambo, a dance form of Cuban origin; his infectious energy and dynamic stage presence quickly made him a star. As his reputation grew, so too did his repertoire, through the addition of other Latin and Afro-Cuban dance rhythms such as Dominican merengue, Brazilian bossa nova, and Cuban cha-cha. The term *salsa* first appeared in the 1960s, when it was used to describe the music that had been the mainstay of Puente's repertoire for decades. Although salsa—as a specific genre—is rooted in the Cuban *son* music, the term has often been applied generically to a wide variety of popularized Latin dance forms, such as those performed by Puente. Aside from his activities as a bandleader and instrumentalist, Puente also wrote many songs, among which "Babarabatiri," "Ran Kan Kan," and "Oye Como Va" have been the most popular.

In the course of his career, Puente recorded some 120 albums and maintained a busy performance schedule, appearing with leading jazz musicians such as George Shearing and Woody Herman, as well as with many stars of Latin music and, in later years, with symphony orchestras. He also performed in several films, including *Radio Days* (1987) and *The Mambo Kings* (1992), and was responsible for introducing American audiences to a number of Latin musicians, most notably Cuban singer Celia Cruz. Puente received five Grammy Awards as well as numerous other honours, and he played 200 to 300 engagements a year until shortly before his death on May 31, 2000, in New York City.

RADIOHEAD

R adiohead is a British rock group that was arguably the most accomplished art-rock band of the early 21st century. This revered quintet made some of the most majestic—if most angst-saturated—music of the postmodern era. Formed in the mid-1980s at Abingdon School in Oxfordshire, Radiohead comprised singer-guitarist Thom Yorke (b. Oct. 7, 1968, Wellingborough, Northamptonshire, England), bassist Colin Greenwood (b. June 26, 1969, Oxford, Oxfordshire), guitarist Ed O'Brien (b. Apr. 15, 1968, Oxford), drummer Phil Selway (b. May 23, 1967, Hemingford Grey, Huntingdon, Cambridgeshire), and guitarist-keyboardist Jonny Greenwood (b. Nov. 5, 1971, Oxford).

Strongly influenced by American bands such as R.E.M. and the Pixies, Radiohead paid early dues on the local pub circuit. With their university education completed, the group landed a deal with Parlophone in late 1991. Although their debut album, *Pablo Honey* (1993), barely hinted at the grandeur to come, the startling single "Creep"—a grungy snarl of self-loathing—made major waves in the United States.

The Bends (1995) took even the band's most ardent fans by surprise. A soaring, intense mix of the approaches of Nirvana and dramatic vocalist Jeff Buckley, the album's powerful sense of alienation completely transcended the parochial issues of mid-1990s Britpop. Driving rockers such as "Bones" were skillfully offset by forlorn ballads such as "High and Dry." The widely acclaimed *OK Computer* (1997) was nothing short of a premillennial version of Pink Floyd's classic album *Dark Side of the Moon* (1973): huge-sounding and chillingly beautiful, with Yorke's weightless voice enveloped on masterpieces such as "Lucky" by webs of dark, dense textures. In its live performances, Radiohead became one of pop music's most compelling acts.

The pressure to follow up one of the most acclaimed recordings of the 20th century told particularly on Yorke's fragile psyche. The band made false starts in Paris and Copenhagen before settling down back in England. When *Kid A* came out in October 2000, it signaled that Radiohead—and Yorke above all—wanted to leave the wide-screen drama of *OK Computer* behind. The resulting selection of heavily electronic, more or less guitar-free pieces (notably "Kid A" and "Idioteque") confounded many but repaid the patience of fans who stuck with it. Though the album was a commercial success, it initially met with mixed critical reaction, as would the similar *Amnesiac* (2001), produced during the same sessions as Kid A. But if Radiohead had seemingly disavowed its musical past on these two albums—moving away from melody and rock instrumentation to create intricately textured soundscapes— it found a way to meld this approach with its guitar-band roots on the much-anticipated album *Hail to the Thief* (2003), which reached number three on the U.S. album charts. In 2006 Yorke, who had reluctantly become for some the voice of his generation, collaborated with the group's modernist producer, Nigel Godrich, on a solo album, *The Eraser*.

The band, having concluded its six-album contract with the EMI Group in 2003, broke away from major label distribution and initially released its seventh album, *In Rainbows* (2007), via Internet download. An estimated 1.2 million fans downloaded the album within its first week of availability, paying any price they wished to do so. The novel distribution method generated headlines, but it was the album's content—a collection of 10 tracks that served as a confident, almost optimistic, sonic counterpoint to *The Bends*—that led critics to declare it the most approachable Radiohead album in a decade.

In Rainbows was released to retailers as a standard CD in 2008, and it immediately hit number one in both the United States and Great Britain; Radiohead also put out a box set that featured CD and vinyl copies of the original tracks, a CD of eight bonus songs, and a booklet of original artwork. After winning its third Grammy Award for the album, the group released the 2009 single "Harry Patch (In Memory Of)," a tribute to one of Britain's last surviving World War I veterans.

The group's eighth release, *The King of Limbs* (2011), debuted using the same online distribution model as *In Rainbows*, but it adhered to a standard pricing model rather than a "pay what you wish" system. The album's title was a reference to a 1,000-year-old oak tree in Wiltshire's Savernake Forest, and its eight tracks played on the interaction of technology and the natural world.

As Radiohead entered its third decade as recording artists, its members often pursued projects outside the context of the band. Yorke, for instance, sang for the electronic-influenced group Atoms for Peace, which in 2013 released the intricately textured *Amok*, while Jonny Greenwood composed film sound tracks.

JIMMIE RODGERS

(b. 1897–d. 1933)

U.S. singer, songwriter, and guitarist Jimmie Rodgers was known throughout his brief six-year recording career as the "Singing Brakeman." His more than 110 recordings made between 1927 and 1933, including "Blue Yodel No. 1," "Brakeman's Blues," "Mississippi River Blues," and "My Time Ain't Long," helped establish the country and western genre. Rodgers became known as "the Father of Country Music."

James Charles Rodgers was born on Sept. 8, 1897, in Pine Springs Community, near Meridian, Miss. His mother died when he was young, and Rodgers spent his youth with various relatives before returning to his father, a foreman on the Mobile and Ohio Railroad, in Meridian. The young Rodgers organized several traveling shows in his early teens, only to be dragged home by his father, who found the 14-year-old work as a water carrier on the railroad. Rodgers subsequently held a number of jobs with the railroad, including brakeman. The life of the railroad worker provided him ample opportunity to develop and exercise his musical skills. He learned to play the guitar and banjo, absorbed the techniques of the blues (from the African American railroad workers), and honed what became his characteristic sound—a blend of traditional country, work, blues, hobo and cowboy songs, as well as yodeling.

After contracting tuberculosis about 1924, Rodgers's condition made it difficult for him to continue to work on the railroad, so he became a medicine-show performer while making a few unsuccessful attempts to return to the railroad. Rodgers moved to Asheville, N.C., in 1927, where he and a group of Tennessee musicians called the Tenneva Ramblers performed on the radio. The group auditioned for Ralph Peer, who was scouting talent for the Victor Talking Machine Company, and the moderate success of the recordings from Rodgers's first session encouraged Rodgers to head to New Jersey for a recording session. His second session produced the song "Away Out on the Mountain," which sold 500,000 copies. Rodgers's use of yodeling to add to a song's mood was nearly as important as his lyrics. He toured mostly in the South and eventually settled in Texas. Ravaged by tuberculosis, Rodgers died on May 26, 1933, in New York City.

THE ROLLING STONES

W ild stage antics and brutal lyrics were the trademarks of one of the most enduring rock music groups. The Rolling Stones, named after a Muddy Waters song, were formed in London, England, in 1962 and by the late 1960s called themselves the World's Greatest Rock and Roll Band.

The Rolling Stones—lead vocalist Mick Jagger (b. Michael Phillip Jagger; July 26, 1942, in Dartford, England); guitarist-vocalist Keith Richards (b. Dec. 18, 1943, in Dartford); guitarist Brian Jones (b. Lewis Brian Hopkins-Jones; Feb. 28, 1942, in Cheltenham, England–d. July 3, 1969); bass player Bill Wyman (b. William Perks; Oct. 24, 1936, in London, England); and drummer Charlie Watts (b. June 2, 1941, in Islington, England)—were formed in London in 1962 by Jagger and Richards, who had attended primary school together. When they became reacquainted ten years after primary school, the pair discovered they shared a love of the blues and began jamming together. They hooked up with Jones, who had drifted around as a musician, and formed a loose-knit group they called the Rolling Stones.

With the later addition of several other musicians, including Bill Wyman and Charlie Watts, the band began performing at a London club. The Rolling Stones were promoted as the wayward counterpart to the hugely successful fellow British band the Beatles. The Stones' debut single, a version of Chuck Berry's "Come On" (1963), was followed by "I Wanna Be Your Man," written by Beatles John Lennon and Paul McCartney. By the time the Stones released the number one hit "It's All Over Now" (1964), they had become a sensation in Britain. Their version of the blues standard "Little Red Rooster," banned in the United States, became another number one hit in Britain.

Throughout the mid-1960s the Stones released a string of hits, including "Time Is on My Side" (1964), "The Last Time" (1965), "Get Off

The Rolling Stones. *Paul Natkin/Archive Photos/Getty Images*

of My Cloud" (1965), "As Tears Go By" (1965), "Satisfaction" (1965), "19th Nervous Breakdown" (1966), "Mother's Little Helper" and "Have You Seen Your Mother, Baby, Standing in the Shadow?" (1966). Throughout their early years the Rolling Stones sang openly about taboo subjects such as drugs and sex. Their bad-boy image brought about threats of censorship when they performed "Let's Spend the Night Together" on *The Ed Sullivan Show* in 1967.

Despite achieving great commercial success, the group was experiencing internal turmoil. Brian Jones announced plans to leave the Stones and form his own group; shortly thereafter, on July 3, 1969, he was found dead in his swimming pool. His replacement, guitarist Mick Taylor (b. Jan. 17, 1948, in Welwyn Garden City, England), was replaced in the mid-1970s by guitarist-vocalist Ron Wood (b. June 1, 1947, in Hillingdon, England). The day after Jones was buried, the band released "Honky Tonk Woman," another number one hit. The band received further notoriety in the aftermath of a concert that they gave at California's Altamont Speedway in 1969. During the concert a young man was murdered by members of the Hell's Angels motorcycle gang, who had been hired by the Stones to provide security for the concert. The incident was captured on film and became part of the documentary *Gimme Shelter*.

In the 1970s the band formed their own record company; had Andy Warhol design for them their distinctive lip-and-tongue logo; and released another spate of popular albums, including the hit singles "Brown Sugar" (1971), "Wild Horses" (1971), "Tumbling Dice" (1972), "Angie" (1973), "It's Only Rock 'n Roll (But I Like It)" (1974), "Some Girls" (1978), and "Miss You" (1978).

As the 1980s progressed, the band settled into a more conventional rock and roll mode compared to other up-and-coming bands. After topping the charts with *Emotional Rescue* (1980) and *Tattoo You* (1981), their subsequent studio albums performed unimpressively. Furthermore, Jagger and Richards were at odds for several years, though by the end of the decade they had reunited, producing the platinum-seller *Steel Wheels* (1989).

During the early 1990s several members of the Stones released solo albums, none of which sold particularly well. As a group, the Rolling Stones earned their first Grammy Award for best rock album for *Voodoo Lounge* (1994). They also conducted two lucrative tours, in 1994 and in 1997, the latter to promote their release *Bridges to Babylon*. The Rolling Stones were inducted into the Rock and Roll Hall of Fame in 1989.

ARNOLD SCHOENBERG

(b. 1874–d. 1951)

The founder of the second Viennese school of musical composition (the first Viennese school is that of Joseph Haydn and Wolfgang Amadeus Mozart), Arnold Schoenberg was one of the most innovative and influential composers of the 20th century. He is credited with the invention of serialism, or 12-tone music, though it was used earlier by Charles Ives and others. A "method of composing with twelve notes [the chromatic scale] related only to one another," it is a form of atonality, or absence of reference to a key or tonal center. Two major composers were pupils of his—Alban Berg and Anton von Webern.

Arnold Franz Walter Schoenberg was born in Vienna, Austria, on Sept. 13, 1874. He learned to play the violin as a child and later taught himself the cello. Almost entirely self-taught as a composer, he modeled his work after that of Johannes Brahms. His earliest major works, however—the string sextet *Verklärte Nacht* ("Transfigured Night"; 1899) and choral *Gurre-Lieder* (begun in 1900; completed in 1911)—are more indebted to Richard Wagner. The two influences came together in Schoenberg's first two numbered string quartets (1905 and 1908) and in his first chamber symphony (1906).

In 1909 Schoenberg produced his first atonal works—*Three Piano Pieces*, *Five Orchestral Pieces*, and a one-act opera *Erwartung* ("Expectation"). *Pierrot Lunaire* ("Moonstruck Pierrot"), 21 recitations with chamber accompaniment, followed in 1912. From 1920 he became preoccupied with serialism, the serial repetition of tones or other elements of music. In this period he produced such serial works as his *Third Quartet*, *Variations for Orchestra*, and the first two acts of his masterpiece, the opera *Moses und Aron* ("Moses and Aaron").

In 1926 Schoenberg went to Berlin, Germany, to teach at the Prussian Academy of Arts. Because he was a Jew, he was dismissed in 1933. He went first to Paris and then moved to the United States, teaching at the University of California at Los Angeles from 1936 to 1944. The major serial works of his last years are a violin concerto and the *Fourth Quartet* (both 1936), a piano concerto (1942), a string trio (1946), and the unfinished *Moderner Psalm* ("Modern Psalm;" 1950).

From 1907 Schoenberg also painted pictures, exhibiting with the Blue Rider group in 1912. His *Harmonielehre* (*Theory of Harmony*; 1911) was widely influential, as were several later textbooks. Schoenberg died in Los Angeles on July 13, 1951.

FRANZ SCHUBERT

(b. 1797–d. 1828)

One of the originators of the Romantic style, Viennese composer Franz Schubert was also the greatest of the post-classicists. He served as a bridge between the two eras. As a composer of songs Schubert is without a rival. He turned poems into music effortlessly. He wrote eight songs in one day, 146 in a single year, and more than 600 in his lifetime. His compositions brought the art of German songwriting to its peak.

Franz Peter Schubert was born in Himmelpfortgrund, near Vienna, Austria, on Jan. 31, 1797. His father was head of the parish school. Young Schubert learned to play the piano, violin, and viola, and he played the viola in the family string quartet. At seven he became a boy soprano in the village choir. Four years later his singing won him a place in the Vienna court choir—now known as the Vienna Choir Boys—and preparatory school. There he studied with the noted Antonio Salieri. He became first violinist in the school orchestra. He began to compose regularly when he was about 13. When he was 16 his voice changed, and he had to leave the imperial school. He taught until 1818 in his father's school. Then he gave up this work and lived only for music.

Schubert was always poor. He applied twice without success for a position as an orchestral conductor. He wrote several operas in an effort to earn money, but they were never performed. In 1828 his friends arranged a benefit concert of his works. Schubert died in Vienna of typhus on Nov. 19, 1828. He was only 31.

Among Schubert's best-known songs are "Erlkönig" ("The Erlking"), "Der Wanderer" ("The Wanderer"), "Der Doppelgänger" ("The Double"), "Gretchen am Spinnrade" ("Gretchen at the Spinning Wheel"), "An Sylvia" ("Who is Sylvia"), and the song cycles *Die schöne Müllerin* ("The Miller's Beautiful Daughter") and *Winterreise* ("Winter Journey"). He left many incomplete works and fragments in many forms. He completed seven symphonies and other orchestral works and numerous choral works, including seven masses. His chamber music includes 16 string quartets and the well-known *Trout Quintet* for violin, viola, cello, double bass, and piano, and the *String Quintet in C Major*. He also wrote many piano works, including about 20 sonatas.

PETE SEEGER

(b. 1919–)

One of the foremost figures of American folk music, Pete Seeger spent decades popularizing his own brand of pop-folk both as a member of various groups and as a solo performer. His most famous songs—"If I Had a Hammer" and "Where Have All the Flowers Gone?"—became well-known pop-folk classics.

Pete Seeger was born on May 3, 1919, in New York, N.Y. Both his father, a musicologist, and his mother, a violin teacher, were on the faculty of the Juilliard School of Music. By the time he was a teenager, Seeger was adept at playing the ukulele, banjo, and guitar. His interest in folk music began when he visited a folk festival in the southern United States. After attending private schools in Manhattan, Seeger enrolled at Harvard University, where he studied sociology for two years.

In the late 1930s, Seeger worked at the Archive of Folk Song in the Library of Congress and appeared on radio programs. He formed the Almanac Singers with Woody Guthrie, Lee Hays, and Millard Lampell in 1940 and released his debut album, *Talking Union and Other Union Songs* (1941), just as the United States was entering World War II. After serving in the Army, Seeger became the national director of People's Songs, Inc., where he used the term "hootenanny" to describe the group's pro-labor, antifascist songs. In the late 1940s, Seeger formed the Weavers, a quartet known for popularizing such folksongs as "On Top of Old Smokey" and "Goodnight Irene."

A performer with a strong social consciousness, Seeger was blacklisted for his alleged Communist sympathies during the 1950s and was unable to get work on network television for 17 years. Throughout this period, Seeger continued to sing and record though his public appearances were limited. By the early 1960s, Seeger had found a new audience among young Americans who increasingly embraced his commitment to political and social change, especially his opposition to American involvement in the Vietnam War. Seeger's albums during that period, such as *We Shall Overcome* (1963) and *Songs of Struggle and Protest 1930–1950* (1964), reflected his antiwar stance. The Byrds recording of his song "Turn! Turn! Turn!," which became a number one hit in 1965, was a fusion of folk and pop with lyrics adapted from a Biblical passage n *Ecclesiastes*.

An accomplished storyteller, music historian, author, and instructor, Seeger educated and influenced many other performers. He played a pivotal role in popularizing the five-string banjo and introduced a variety of instruments into folk music. In the 1990s he continued to perform before audiences young and old in concerts that typically included active audience participation. He was inducted into the Rock and Roll Hall of Fame in 1996.

THE SEX PISTOLS

The Sex Pistols were a rock group who created the British punk movement of the late 1970s and who, with the song "God Save the Queen," became a symbol of the United Kingdom's social and political turmoil. The original members were Johnny Rotten (byname of John Lydon; b. Jan. 31, 1956, London, Eng.), Steve Jones (b. May 3, 1955, London), Paul Cook (b. July 20, 1956, London), and Glen Matlock (b. Aug. 27, 1956, London). A later member was Sid Vicious (byname of John Simon Ritchie; b. May 10, 1957, London–d. Feb. 2, 1979, New York, N.Y.).

Thrown together in September 1975 by manager Malcolm McLaren to promote Sex, his London clothing store, the Sex Pistols began mixing 1960s English pop music influences—such as the Small Faces and the Who—with those of 1970s rock renegades—Iggy and the Stooges and the New York Dolls—in an attempt to strip rock's complexities to the bone. By the summer of 1976 the Sex Pistols had attracted an avid fan base and successfully updated the energies of the 1960s mods for the malignant teenage mood of the '70s. Media-savvy, ambitious in their use of lyrics, and heavily stylized in their image and music, the Sex Pistols became the leaders of a new teenage movement—called "punk" by the British press—in the autumn of 1976. Their first single, "Anarchy in the U.K.," was both a call to arms and a state-of-the-nation address. When they used profanity on live television in December 1976, the group became a national sensation. Scandalized in the tabloid press, the Sex Pistols were dropped by their first record company, EMI, in January 1977; their next contract, with A&M Records, was severed after only a few days in March.

Signing quickly with Virgin Records, the Sex Pistols released their second single, "God Save the Queen," in June 1977 to coincide with Queen Elizabeth II's Silver Jubilee (the 25th anniversary of her accession to the throne). Although banned by the British media, the single rose rapidly to number two on the charts. As "public enemies number one," the Sex Pistols were subjected to physical violence and harassment.

Despite a second top ten record, "Pretty Vacant," the Sex Pistols stalled. Barely able to play in the United Kingdom because of local government bans, they became mired in preparations for a film and the worsening drug use of Rotten's friend Vicious, who had replaced Matlock in February 1977. Their bunker mentality is evident on their third top ten hit, "Holidays in the Sun." By the time their album *Never Mind the Bollocks, Here's the Sex Pistols* reached number one in early November, Rotten, Vicious, Jones, and Cook had recorded together for the last time.

A short, disastrous U.S. tour precipitated the group's split in January 1978 following their biggest show to date, in San Francisco. Attempting to keep the Sex Pistols going with the film project that became *The Great Rock 'n' Roll Swindle* (1980), McLaren issued records with an increasingly uncontrollable Vicious as the vocalist. A cover version of Eddie Cochran's "C'mon Everybody" became the group's best-selling single following Vicious's fatal heroin overdose in New York City in February 1979 while out on bail (charged with the murder of his girlfriend, Nancy Spungen). That same month McLaren was sued by Rotten, and the Sex Pistols disappeared into receivership, only to be revived some years after the 1986 court case that restored control of their affairs to the group. A reunion tour in 1996 finally allowed the original quartet to play their hit songs in front of supportive audiences. This anticlimactic postscript, however, did not lessen the impact of their first four singles and debut album, which shook the foundations of rock music and sent tremors through British society. In 2006 the Sex Pistols were inducted into the Rock and Roll Hall of Fame.

RAVI SHANKAR

(b. 1920–d. 2012)

Sitar player and composer Ravi Shankar introduced the music of India to Western audiences. His international fame peaked in the 1960s through performances in North America and Europe, the release of several popular recordings, and collaborations with Western classical, jazz, and rock musicians.

Born in the Hindu holy city of Benares (now Varanasi) in India on Apr. 7, 1920, Rabendra (Ravi) Shankar was the youngest of five brothers in a Brahman, or highest caste, Hindu family. At the age of 10, Ravi, with his mother and two brothers, joined an Indian dance troupe in Paris, France, established by his oldest brother, Uday. Ravi lived in Paris for more than five years, attending Roman Catholic schools and performing with the troupe.

With war on the European horizon, Ravi returned to India for seven years of sitar study with master musician Ustad Allauddin Khan. Shankar married Khan's daughter Annapurna in May 1941. In 1944 he moved to Bombay (now Mumbai) to work for the Indian People's Theatre Association. He composed a number of Indian film scores as well as a ballet, *The Discovery of India*, staged in 1947.

The next year Shankar became music director and orchestra conductor for All-India Radio in New Delhi. While his audience grew within India, he was largely unknown abroad until his score for the 1955 film *Pather Panchali*, directed by Satyajit Ray, won awards at the Cannes, Venice, and Berlin film festivals.

Shankar first toured the United States and England in 1956. Over the next decade his audiences grew from small rooms of Asian immigrants to sold-out concerts at New York City's Philharmonic Hall. Sitar music did not fit Western categories. Shankar recorded jazz collaborations with Bud Shank and Paul Horn in the early 1960s. He taught at the University of California in 1965. He and violinist Yehudi Menuhin played together at the Bath Music Festival in England in 1966 and the United Nations in 1967, the year in which they released the collaborative album

West Meets East. Two classes taught by Shankar at the City College of New York in 1967 attracted almost 300 students. Having founded the Kinnara School of Music in Bombay in 1962, he established a Los Angeles branch in 1967.

George Harrison of the Beatles first introduced Shankar to the world of rock music. After using a sitar in "Norwegian Wood" on the 1965 Beatles album *Rubber Soul*, Harrison met Shankar at a London dinner party and arranged to study with him in India in late 1966. The sitar sound spread from the Beatles to other rock groups. Shankar protested the association of Indian

Ravi Shankar playing the sitar. *Deshakalyan Chowdhury/AFP/Getty Images*

classical music with American drugs. At the Monterey Pop Festival in June 1967, the destruction of musical instruments by Jimi Hendrix and the Who upset Shankar so much that he almost refused to play.

Shankar performed in Harrison's Aug. 1971 Concert for Bangladesh and recorded a series of albums in 1972–75 for the Beatles' Apple label and Harrison's Dark Horse label. His many compositions included concertos for sitar and sound tracks for the films *Charly* (1968) and *Gandhi* (1982, with George Fenton). Shankar performed with André Previn and Zubin Mehta. He collaborated with Philip Glass on a 1990 album, *Passages*. George Harrison honored his teacher's 75th birthday in 1995 with a four-CD set, *In Celebration*. Two years later Harrison produced *Chants of India*, featuring Shankar's arrangements of classical Indian music. Shankar died on Dec. 11, 2012, in San Diego, Calif.

DMITRI SHOSTAKOVICH

(b. 1906–d. 1975)

O ne of the greatest modern Soviet composers, Dimitri Shostakovich once stated, "There can be no music without ideology." Because of their political connotations, his works were controversial in both Communist and non-Communist countries. In the Soviet Union his music was either praised for its wit or condemned for "vulgarity."

Dimitri Dimitrievich Shostakovich was born on Sept. 25 [O.S. Sept. 13], 1906, in St. Petersburg, Russia. His mother saw to it that he and his two sisters started piano lessons when they were each nine. Dimitri was a small, rather sickly boy.

He saw much of the excitement and terror of the Russian Revolution in 1917. He entered the Petrograd Conservatory in 1919. For presentation at his graduation, in 1926, he wrote his *Symphony No. 1 in F minor*. It had an enthusiastic reception and remained one of the composer's most consistently popular works.

In his early years Shostakovich was influenced by the music of Aleksander Scriabin, Peter Ilich Tchaikovsky, Johann Sebastian Bach, and Ludwig van Beethoven. Gradually his own style asserted itself. His works include 15 symphonies, many pieces of chamber music, and the scores for ballets, operas, and motion pictures.

In 1948 Joseph Stalin condemned Shostakovich's music for "antidemocratic tendencies...alien to Soviet people and their artistic tastes." After Stalin's death, Shostakovich was honored on his 60th birthday by being the first composer to be named a hero of socialist labor. He died in Moscow on Aug. 9, 1975.

SIMON AND GARFUNKEL

Paul Simon (b. 1941–)
Art Garfunkel (b. 1941–)

U .S. folk duo Paul Simon and Art Garfunkel are renowned entertainers. Born Paul Frederick Simon on Oct. 13, 1941, in Newark,

130

N.J., Simon grew up in Queens, N.Y. He met Art Garfunkel in grade school in the early 1950s, and by high school they had formed a duet called Tom and Jerry. Their first hit single, "Hey Schoolgirl," was recorded while they were still in high school.

Garfunkel (b. Nov. 5, 1941) was raised in the middle-class neighborhood of Forest Hills, N.Y. He began singing at age four when his father, who worked in the garment packaging business, brought home an early tape recorder. He brought his lyrical tenor and high harmonies to the pair's string of hits.

During the early 1960s Simon recorded a number of solo singles under the name Jerry Landis while continuing to work with Garfunkel. Garfunkel, who had also recorded several songs on his own as Arty Garr, preferred to let Simon do the songwriting while he concentrated on arranging. Meanwhile, they had begun performing together in local New York clubs and honing their sound. Eventually the duo started to call themselves Simon and Garfunkel. A Columbia Records executive heard them play at a folk club in New York City's Greenwich Village and signed them.

Their first album, *Wednesday Morning, 3 am* (1964), which included their classic "The Sounds of Silence," was not a commercial success. The album was rereleased two years later as *The Sounds of Silence* (1966), and only then did the title track become a hit. They followed up with a string of hits (and numerous Grammy Awards) including "The Boxer," "Mrs. Robinson," from the film *The Graduate* (1968), "The 59th Street Bridge Song (Feelin' Groovy)," "Scarborough Fair/Canticle," and "Bridge over Troubled Water."

In 1971 Simon and Garfunkel split, though they continued to perform and record together on occasion throughout their individual solo careers. Throughout the 1970s Simon had one hit after another and earned a Grammy Award. As a successful solo artist, Simon distinguished himself from other folk-based artists with a musical style as unique and expressive as his lyrics. Experimenting with a variety of musical styles— including rock, jazz, reggae, salsa, blues, gospel, New Orleans, South African, and Brazilian—he created his own blend of pop, showcasing world music a decade before the term became a common musical category. Following the failure of his Broadway play *The Capeman* in 1998,

Simon began work on the album *You're the One*, which was nominated for a Grammy in 2001. Simon was inducted into the Rock and Roll Hall of Fame as a solo performer in 2001. In 2007 he became the first recipient of the Library of Congress Gershwin Prize for Popular Song.

After the split with Simon, Garfunkel did not record again until 1973. His solo debut *Angel Clare* (1973) included the hit single of Jimmy Webb's "All I Know" and earned him a gold disc. *Breakaway* (1975), his second album, did even better, earning him a platinum disc. In addition to the title song the album featured "I Only Have Eyes for You" and reunited Garfunkel with Simon for "My Little Town." In 1978 Garfunkel teamed with Simon and James Taylor for a hit version of Sam Cooke's "(What a) Wonderful World." He also made his first solo tour in the United States.

Both artists continued to record solo albums and perform both solo and together. The duo was inducted into the Rock and Roll Hall of Fame in 1990.

FRANK SINATRA

(b. 1915–d. 1998)

The term "bobby-soxers" was first used in 1943–44 to identify the young audiences who sighed, squealed, sobbed, and swooned over Frankie Boy—the original teen idol. Part of Frank Sinatra's appeal then was his vulnerable, slouchy look, and part was his way of caressing a lyric. He bent his voice like a trombone to develop an intimate style of provocative slurs and eccentric phrasing. Known to different generations as the Voice, Ol' Blue Eyes, and Chairman of the Board, he was a superstar for more than five decades.

Francis Albert Sinatra was born on Dec. 12, 1915, in Hoboken, N.J., the only child of Martin Sinatra and Natalie (Garavante) Sinatra, both native Italians. Sinatra briefly worked as a copy boy for a local newspaper before he decided to pursue a singing career. He began singing in amateur shows in 1933 and formed a musical group, the Hoboken Four. By 1938 Sinatra was touring with a travel-ing radio show and performing at clubs and roadhouses. Bandleader Harry James discovered Sinatra's act at the Rustic Cabin in New Jersey in 1939. Their best recording together, "All or Nothing at All," did not become a hit until after the singer's solo career took off four years later.

During 1940–42 Sinatra developed his style with trombonist Tommy Dorsey's band. As a gifted interpreter of popular standards, Sinatra was highly sensitive to the lyrics of the songs he sang. Exquisitely long phrases and delicate nuance of emotion distinguished his trade-mark style. Sinatra's popularity grew with such hits as "I'll Never Smile Again," "Night and Day," "This Love of Mine," and "There Are Such Things." Once drawing mainly young audiences, Sinatra gained a cross-generational following through an engagement with the Benny Goodman orchestra at New York City's Paramount Theater in 1942–43. These landmark performances marked the launch of Sinatra's career as a solo artist. From 1943 to 1945 Sinatra was the lead singer on the radio program *Your Hit Parade* and began recording for Columbia Records.

Sinatra made his motion-picture debut in the 1943 musical *Higher and Higher*. He would go on to play diverse roles in more than 50 films. He won his first Academy Award in 1945 for the patriotic short sub-ject *The House I Live In*. Suffering from severely damaged vocal chords, Sinatra hit a low point in his career in the early 1950s. *From Here to Eternity* (1953), based on James Jones's best-selling novel about United States servicemen in Hawaii on the eve of World War II, brought Sinatra an Oscar for best supporting actor and helped revitalize his slumping career. He was nominated for best actor for *The Man with the Golden Arm* (1955). Other films included *Suddenly* (1954), *Pal Joey* (1957), *The Manchurian Candidate* (1962), *The Detective* (1968), and *The First Deadly Sin* (1980). Throughout the 1960s Sinatra made comedies with fellow members of the high-living show-business clique nicknamed the Rat Pack, which included Dean Martin and Sammy Davis, Jr. These films included *Ocean's Eleven* (1960) and *Robin and the Seven Hoods* (1964). Sinatra also made numerous appearances on television.

After his first marriage to childhood sweetheart Nancy Barbato ended in divorce, Sinatra married actress Ava Gardner in 1951. The marriage was tempestuous, and they separated and eventually divorced in 1957. Sinatra staged a comeback as a recording artist in 1953 when he left Columbia Records for Capitol Records and began collaborating with conductor-arranger Nelson Riddle. Riddle's up-tempo arrangements showcased Sinatra's new "swinging" style, which was both more aggressive and alluring. Up against immensely popular rock and roll musicians of the era, Sinatra scored hits with the albums *In the Wee Small Hours* (1955), *Songs for Swingin' Lovers* (1956), and *Frank Sinatra Sings for Only the Lonely* (1958). *Come Dance With Me!* (1959) won Sinatra his first Grammy Awards, for album of the year and best male vocal performance.

In 1960 Sinatra founded the record label Reprise Records. His singing style continued to evolve, growing brasher and punchier. The album *September of My Years* (1965) won Grammy Awards for album of the year and best male vocal performance. In 1966 *A Man and His Music* was voted album of the year, and "Strangers in the Night" became a number one single. With hit songs such as "That's Life" (1966) and "My Way" (1969), Sinatra drew sold-out crowds to Madison Square Garden and the Forum in Los Angeles, Calif. He also performed in Las Vegas, Nev., as did his fellow Rat Packers. Actress Mia Farrow and Sinatra were married in 1966; they divorced two years later.

Sinatra briefly stopped performing in 1971, but he announced his return with the album *Ol' Blue Eyes Is Back* (1973). Sinatra married Barbara Marx, the former wife of Zeppo Marx, in 1976. Another Sinatra classic, "New York, New York" (1980), a cover version of the Liza Minnelli song from the 1977 film of the same name, emerged during the later years of Sinatra's musical career. Frequent concert work included the Ultimate Event tour (1989–90) with Minnelli and Sammy Davis, Jr. The album *Duets* (1993), on which Sinatra sang with younger pop music artists, sold more than two million copies in the United States. At the 1994 Grammy Awards Sinatra was honored for a lifetime of musical achievement. In 1996 he won a final Grammy Award for the album *Duets II*. By the end of his singing career, Sinatra had received nine Grammy Awards. He gave his final live performance in California on Feb. 25, 1995. On May 14, 1998, Sinatra died of a heart attack in Los Angeles, Calif.

BESSIE SMITH

(b. 1894–d. 1937)

O ne of the greatest of the blues singers, Bessie Smith sang of the cares and troubles she had known—of poverty and oppression, of love and indifference. Her art is known today through the more than 150 songs she recorded during her brief career.

Bessie Smith was born on April 15, probably in 1894, in Chattanooga, Tenn. Her family was poor, and she got her start as a singer with the help of Ma Rainey, one of the first great professional blues vocalists. Rainey organized troupes of musicians and dancers and led them on tours of the South and the Midwest.

Smith was discovered by a record company representative—the pianist and composer Clarence Williams. She made her first recordings— "Downhearted Blues" and "Gulf Coast Blues"—in February 1923. These sold very well, and by the end of 1925 she had made a number of successful recordings, some of them accompanied by the trumpet playing of the legendary Louis Armstrong.

Smith's great popularity continued through the 1920s, and in 1929 she made a short motion picture, *Saint Louis Blues*. Then, with the 1930s and the Great Depression, public taste began to change. The blues lost some of their appeal, and blues recordings did not sell very well. Smith continued singing, appearing at clubs in Philadelphia, Pa., and New York City and varying her act by introducing popular songs among the blues numbers. She also became increasingly dependent on alcohol, which made it more difficult for her to find work. While traveling in Mississippi, Smith was seriously injured in an automobile accident. She died on Sept. 26, 1937, while being taken to the hospital in Clarksdale, Miss.

Smith's recordings, which have been collected into albums, remain popular. Her work influenced a number of successful singers, including Billie Holiday, Mahalia Jackson, and Janis Joplin.

SMOKEY ROBINSON AND THE MIRACLES

Smokey Robinson and the Miracles were an American vocal group that helped define the Motown sound of the 1960s were led by one of the most gifted and influential singer-songwriters in 20th-century popular music. In addition to Smokey Robinson, byname of William Robinson (b. Feb. 19, 1940, Detroit, Mich.), the principal members of the group were Warren Moore (b. Nov. 19, 1939, Detroit), Bobby Rogers (b. Feb. 19, 1940, Detroit–d. March 3, 2013, Southfield, Mich.), Ronnie White (b. Apr. 5, 1939, Detroit), and Claudette Rogers (b. Sept. 1, 1942). Whether writing for fellow artists Mary Wells, the Temptations, or Marvin Gaye or performing with the Miracles, singer-lyricist-arranger-producer Robinson created songs that were supremely balanced between the joy and pain of love. At once playful and passionate, Robinson's graceful lyrics led Bob Dylan to call him "America's greatest living poet."

Coming of age in the doo-wop era and deeply influenced by jazz vocalist Sarah Vaughan, Robinson formed the Five Chimes with school friends in the mid-1950s. After some personnel changes, the group, as the Matadors, auditioned unsuccessfully for Jackie Wilson's manager. However, they greatly impressed Wilson's songwriter Berry Gordy, who soon became their manager and producer. Most importantly, Gordy became Robinson's mentor, harnessing his prodigious but unformed composing talents, and Robinson, assisted by the Miracles, became Gordy's inspiration for the creation of Motown Records.

With the arrival of Claudette Rogers, the group changed its name to the Miracles and released "Got a Job" on End Records in 1958. The Miracles struggled onstage in their first performance at the Apollo Theatre that year, but good fortune came their way in the form of Marv Tarplin (b. June 13, 1941, Atlanta, Ga.–d. Sept. 30, 2011, Las Vegas, Nev.), guitarist for the Primettes, who were led by Robinson's friend Diana Ross. Tarplin became an honorary (but essential) Miracle, while

Robinson introduced Gordy to the Primettes, who soon became the Supremes. In 1959 Robinson and Claudette Rogers were married, and "Bad Girl," licensed to Chess Records, peaked nationally at number 93. The fiery "Way Over There" and the shimmering "(You Can) Depend on Me" were followed in 1960 by "Shop Around," the second version of which became an enormous hit, reaching number one on the rhythm-and-blues charts and number two on the pop charts.

While Robinson was writing such vital songs as "My Guy" for Mary Wells, "I'll Be Doggone" for Marvin Gaye, and "My Girl" for the Temptations, he and the Miracles proceeded to record stunning compositions, including "You've Really Got a Hold on Me" (1962), "I'll Try Something New" (1962), "Ooo Baby Baby" (1965), "Choosey Beggar" (1965), "The Tracks of My Tears" (1965), and "More Love" (1967, written following the premature birth and death of Robinson's twin daughters). The Miracles complemented their songs of aching romance and mature love with buoyant numbers such as "Mickey's Monkey" (1963), "Going to a Go-Go" (1965), "I Second That Emotion" (1967), and "The Tears of a Clown" (1970).

In 1972 Robinson left the Miracles to pursue a solo career. Without him the Miracles enjoyed moderate success in subsequent years—the disco-era "Love Machine (Part 1)" hit number one on the pop charts in 1975—while Robinson produced such solo hits as "Cruisin'" (1979) and "Being with You" (1981). He also unintentionally inspired the new soul radio format that took its name from the title track of his 1975 conceptual album *A Quiet Storm*. Robinson was inducted into the Rock and Roll Hall of Fame in 1987. The Miracles were inducted in 2012.

BRUCE SPRINGSTEEN

(b. 1949–)

Known to his fans as the Boss, Springsteen became a music superstar and an unparalleled pop phenomenon in the mid-1980s. Springsteen's four-hour-long concerts sold out in outdoor stadiums around the world and his album *Born in the U.S.A.* sold more than 15 million copies.

Bruce Springsteen was born in Freehold, N.J., on Sept. 23, 1949. He bought his first guitar at the age of 13 after seeing Elvis Presley perform on television. He joined his first band a year later. After dropping out of a local community college, Springsteen formed and played in several bands. In the early 1970s he formed the E Street Band, which gained a loyal following in the Northeast.

Springsteen's first two albums, *Greetings from Asbury Park, N.J.* (1973) and *The Wild, The Innocent and the E Street Shuffle* (1973), increased his cult following, and a widely quoted review in 1974 described him as "rock and roll future." It was not until the release of *Born to Run* (1975) and his first national tour, however, that he gained widespread attention. Springsteen's early music often took as its theme a love for cars and the frustrations of urban adolescence.

Bruce Springsteen reaches out to fans in the audience as he performs. *Mark Metcalfe/ Getty Images*

Darkness on the Edge of Town (1978), *The River* (1980), and the solo album *Nebraska* (1982) preceded *Born in the U.S.A.* (1984). Springsteen's raspy voice, his concern for the working class, and his simple, emotional lyrics appealed to a wide audience. A five-record collection of live performances, *Bruce Springsteen and the E Street Band Live 1975/1985* (1986), was followed by *Tunnel of Love* (1987).

In late 1989, following his Tunnel of Love tour, Springsteen disbanded the E Street Band. After a five-year hiatus from recording he released the pop-oriented *Human Touch* (1992) and *Lucky Town* (1993), which explored his feelings about parenting and adulthood. His hit single "Streets of Philadelphia" (1994), featured on the sound track of the film *Philadelphia*, earned him four Grammys and an Academy Award. Springsteen's *Greatest Hits* album (1995), which contained four previously unreleased songs, debuted at number one on the Billboard charts, becoming his twelfth platinum album. His subsequent release, the more personal and serious *The Ghost of Tom Joad* (1995), which examined the plight of immigrants in the United States, had mixed reviews and was Springsteen's first album not to go platinum, though it eventually earned a Grammy for best contemporary folk album.

Springsteen contributed music to the sound track for the feature film *Dead Man Walking* (1996) as well as to the celebrity-packed album *The Concert for the Rock and Roll Hall of Fame* (1996). Preferring midsize venues to the massive concert halls he formerly played, Springsteen embarked on a major U.S. and world tour in 1996–97, his first solo acoustic theater tour in more than a decade.

Springsteen was married to model and actress Julianne Phillips from 1985 until 1989. He married his former backup singer Patti Scialfa in 1991.

IGOR STRAVINSKY

(b. 1882–d. 1971)

One of the giants in 20th-century musical composition, Russian-born Igor Stravinsky was both original and influential. He restored a healthy unwavering pulse essential to ballet; he was meticulous about degrees of articulation and emphasis; he created a "clean" sound, with no filling in merely for the sake of filling in; he wrote for different instrumental groupings and created a different sound in every work; he revived musical forms from the past; and he made a lasting contribution to serial, or 12-tone, music.

Igor Fyodorovich Stravinsky was born on June 17 [O.S. June 5], 1882, in Oranienbaum, near St. Petersburg, Russia, the son of the leading bass at the Russian Imperial Opera. Although he was taught piano, harmony, and counterpoint as a child, his family determined that he would have a career in law, and he graduated from St. Petersburg University in 1905. He had met the composer Nikolai Rimski-Korsakov in 1902 and from 1903 to 1906 studied privately with him—mainly instrumentation and analysis. Through the influence of Rimski-Korsakov, Stravinsky's early works including *Symphony in E-flat*, *Feu d-artifice* (Fireworks), and *Scherzo fantastique* received performances. The ballet impresario Sergei Diaghilev heard the performances and engaged Stravinsky to orchestrate various pieces of ballet music for the 1909 season of his Ballets Russes in Paris. This began a long collaboration, which produced such major works as *L'oiseau de feu* (*The Firebird*; 1910), *Pétrouchka* (*Petrushka*; 1911), *Le Sacre du printemps* (*The Rite of Spring*; 1913), *Pulcinella* (1920), and *Les noces* (*The Wedding*; 1923).

In his early years with the Ballets Russes, Stravinsky spent more and more time outside Russia, and with the advent of World War I he lived in Switzerland. During these years he produced two strikingly original stage works—*Renard* ("The Fox"; 1916), "a burlesque in song and dance," and *Histoire du soldat* (*The Soldier's Tale*; 1918), "to be read, played, and danced."

After the war Stravinsky moved to France, where he developed subsidiary careers as a concert pianist and conductor. He performed as soloist in some of his new works such as *Concerto for Piano and Wind Instruments* (1924), *Capriccio for Piano and Orchestra* (1929), and *Concerto for Two Solo Pianos* (1935). The French years marked a major change in Stravinsky's style—from basically Russian influences to a neoclassical idiom. The two peaks of this period are the opera-oratorio *Oedipus rex* (1927) and the *Symphony of Psalms* (1930).

Invited to lecture at Harvard University in 1939, Stravinsky moved to the United States, making his home in Hollywood, Calif. The war years produced the *Symphony in C*, the summation of neoclassical principles in symphonic form, and *Symphony in Three Movements*, which combines features of the concerto with the symphony.

From 1948 to 1951 Stravinsky worked on his neoclassical opera, *The Rake's Progress*, conducting its first performance in Venice, Italy. He engaged the young American musician Robert Craft to help him in Hollywood, and through Craft became interested in serial music—particularly that of Anton von Webern. His *Canticum Sacrum* for voices and orchestra (1955) and ballet *Agon* contain 12-tone elements and were followed by the fully serial works *Threni* (1958), *Movements* (1959), *Variations* (1964), and *Requiem Canticles* (1966).

Ill health slowed Stravinsky in his final years, and he died in New York City on Apr. 6, 1971. He was buried in Venice on the island of San Michele.

PETER ILICH TCHAIKOVSKY

(b. 1840–d. 1893)

Few composers have put as much of themselves into their work as Peter Ilich Tchaikovsky. A shy man, he expressed his emotions in music.

Tchaikovsky was born on May 7 [O.S. April 25], 1840, in Votkinsk in the Ural Mountains. He began taking piano lessons at the age of seven. When the family moved to St. Petersburg in 1850, young Tchaikovsky enrolled in the School of Laws. In 1859 he graduated and became a clerk in the Ministry of Justice.

Tchaikovsky turned more and more to music. In 1861 he began to study with Anton Rubinstein. Five years later he became a teacher at the Moscow Conservatory. During his years there, Tchaikovsky composed some of his most famous works. They include the ballet *Lebedinoye ozero* (*Swan Lake*), the overture *Romeo and Juliet*, the instrumental fantasy *Francesca da Rimini*, and the popular *First Piano Concerto*. Many of his early compositions were coldly received. However, Nadezhda von Meck, a wealthy widow, had complete faith in his talent. Beginning in 1877 she gave him encouragement and money. For 13 years they wrote each other long letters, though they never met.

141

In 1877 Tchaikovsky also met Antonina Milyukova, a young music student who had declared her love for him. Feeling social and familial pressures, the unhappy Tchaikovsky agreed to marry her. After just a few weeks, however, their total lack of compatibility led Tchaikovsky to flee abroad, never again to live with his wife.

Shortly after they began to correspond, von Meck persuaded Tchaikovsky to accept a yearly allowance. This enabled the composer to give up teaching. Living quietly abroad or at his sister's estate near Kiev, he composed steadily, including his notable violin concerto. Many of his themes were taken from Russian folk tunes. By 1880 he was the most popular composer in Russia. In 1887 he conducted publicly for the first time. European concert tours followed, but intense homesickness and stage fright kept his life miserable.

In 1891 Tchaikovsky made a concert tour in the United States. On his return to Russia he completed the *Shchelkunchik, Balet-feyeriya* (*Nutcracker Suite*) and his *Symphony No. 6*, usually called the *Pathétique*. While in St. Petersburg for the symphony's first performance, Tchaikovsky contracted cholera. He died there on November 6 [O.S. October 25], 1893.

U2

The Irish rock band U2 had established itself by the end of the 1980s not only as one of the world's most popular bands but also as one of the most innovative. Though forged in the crucible of punk rock that swept Europe in the late 1970s, U2 instantly created a distinctive identity with its grandiose sound.

The members of U2 included vocalist Bono (byname of Paul Hewson; b. May 10, 1960, Dublin, Ire.), guitarist the Edge (byname of David Evans; b. Aug. 8, 1961, Barking, Essex [now in Greater London], England), bassist Adam Clayton (b. March 13, 1960, Oxford, Oxfordshire, England), and drummer Larry Mullen, Jr. (b. Oct. 31, 1961, Dublin). The four were attending a Dublin high school when they began rehearsing together, undeterred by their lack of technical expertise. The band's early albums, including the less than well-received *October* (1981), were characterized

U2 onstage. *Dave J Hogan/Getty Images*

by an intense spirituality, and they commented on social and political issues, such as the civil strife in Northern Ireland, with compassion and tenderness. With the live album *Under a Blood Red Sky* (1983), featuring the hit "Sunday Bloody Sunday," the group became renowned for its inspirational live performances. A few years later, with the multimillion-selling success of *The Joshua Tree* (1987) and the number one hits "With or Without You" and "I Still Haven't Found What I'm Looking For," U2 became pop stars. They followed *The Joshua Tree* with *Rattle and Hum* (1988), a double album and documentary movie exploring blues, country, gospel, and folk music.

U2 reinvented itself for the new decade, reemerging in 1991 with the album *Achtung Baby* and a sound heavily influenced by European experimental, electronic, and disco music. The 1992 Zoo TV tour was a technically ambitious and artistically accomplished large-scale rock spectacle. The subsequent albums *Zooropa* (1993) and *Pop* (1997) were

143

also recorded in the same electronica/disco vein. The band returned to their 1980s roots with *All That You Can't Leave Behind* (2000), which won multiple Grammy Awards, *How to Dismantle an Atomic Bomb* (2004) and *No Line on the Horizon* (2009). U2 was elected into the Rock and Roll Hall of Fame in 2005.

GIUSEPPE VERDI

(b. 1813–d. 1901)

O ne of the leading composers of Italian operas in the 19th century was Giuseppe Verdi. His *Rigoletto* (1851), *Il trovatore* ("The Troubador"; 1853) and *La traviata* ("The Strayed Woman"; 1853), and *Aïda* (1871) will be staged as long as operas are performed.

Giuseppe Verdi was born on Oct. 9 or 10, 1813, in Le Roncole, a village near Parma in northern Italy's Po River valley. The child of a poor family, Verdi showed unusual musical talent at an early age. A local amateur musician named Antonio Barezzi helped him with his education. At Barezzi's expense he was sent to Milan when he was 18. He stayed there for three years, then served as musical director in Busseto for two years before returning to Milan. By 1840, just as he had established a reputation and begun to make money, he was discouraged by personal tragedies. Within a three-year period his wife and both of his children died.

In his nearly 30 operas, Verdi's music shapes and advances the dramatic action. He often links musical themes and motifs with specific characters and events, especially in such late masterpieces as *Otello* (1887) and *Falstaff* (1893). The emotional impact, drama, and soaring melodies that characterize his operas are also found in such nonoperatic works as his *Requiem* and *Four Sacred Pieces*.

With his opera *Ernani* (1844), Verdi's fame and fortune were made. The right to publish one opera brought him $4,000. Later he received $20,000 for the first night's performance of *Aïda*. Verdi's last opera, *Falstaff*, was produced just before his 80th birthday. Thousands of music lovers journeyed to Milan from all parts of Italy for its first performance, and the ovation the aged composer received has seldom been equaled in musical history. He died in Milan on Jan. 27, 1901. A Verdi museum has been established in La Scala opera house in Milan to honor his work there.

ANTONIO VIVALDI

(b. 1678–d. 1741)

The most influential and innovative Italian composer of his time, Antonio Vivaldi was an accomplished violinist who wrote music for operas, solo instruments, and small ensembles. His finest work was thought to be his concerti in which virtuoso solo passages alternate with passages for the whole orchestra. He orchestrated in new ways and prepared the way for the late baroque concerto.

Antonio Lucio Vivaldi was born on March 4, 1678, in Venice, Italy. When he was born he looked so frail that the midwife baptized him immediately. He grew to love the violin and played along with his father at St. Mark's Basilica. The young Vivaldi studied for the priesthood and was ordained in 1703. The same year, he was given a teaching position at the Pio Ospedale della Pietà, where he gave music lessons to those among the resident orphan girls who showed musical aptitude. Their Sunday concerts, for which Vivaldi composed many orchestral and choral works, gained renown, until no visit to Venice was considered complete without hearing a performance.

Vivaldi taught there until 1709, when for financial reasons the school voted not to renew his post. Two years later he was reappointed, however, and he remained as a teacher until 1716, when he was appointed to the higher position of maestro. In his later years Vivaldi traveled widely, living for extended periods in Vienna and Mantua, where he was the director of secular music for the city's governor, Prince Philip of Hesse-Darmstadt. He probably also performed and composed in Prague, Dresden, and Amsterdam. His popularity declined at the end of his life, and he died in Vienna on July 28, 1741.

Early in his life Vivaldi's operas were performed throughout Italy and in Vienna. More than 750 works are known to exist, and researchers have long struggled with the task of identifying and cataloguing them. Vivaldi's original musical style had wide influence on later composers, including Johann Sebastian Bach, who transcribed some of Vivaldi's concerti for keyboard. His operas are seldom heard now, but his orchestral and chamber music are performed frequently, as is his popular sacred *Gloria*.

RICHARD WAGNER

(b. 1813–d. 1883)

A mong the great composers for the theater, Richard Wagner was the only one who created plot, characters, text, and symbolism as well as the music. He raised the melodic and harmonic style of German music to its highest emotional intensity, changing the course of Western music by either the extension of his methods or the reaction against them.

Wilhelm Richard Wagner was born in Leipzig, Germany, on May 22, 1813. Inspired by the works of composers such as Beethoven, Mozart, and Weber, as well as writers, including Shakespeare, Goethe, and Schiller, he taught himself piano and composition. He entered the University of Leipzig, living wildly but applying himself seriously to composition. His *Symphony in C major* was performed in Prague in 1832 and the following year in Leipzig.

The next six years he spent as a conductor at third-rate provincial theaters. In 1836 he married the actress Minna Planer, and in 1839, fleeing creditors, they left for Paris. Living among poor German artists, he wrote musical journalism and did hack work. But in 1840 he completed *Rienzi*, his first significant opera. It was successfully produced at Dresden in 1842 and resulted in his appointment as musical director of the Saxon court. Here *Der fliegende Holländer* (*The Flying Dutchman*) was produced in 1843, and *Tannhäuser* was completed in 1845. They were much criticized, for they lacked the tuneful melodies of the popular opera.

Wagner took part in the German political revolt of 1848–49 and was forced to leave the country. For about ten years he lived in Zürich,

Switzerland. In 1864 King Ludwig II of Bavaria invited him to continue his musical work in Munich. During the years in Munich, he completed *Der Ring des Nibelungen* (*The Ring of the Nibelung*), a series of operas based on old German myths that he had begun in Zürich.

The opera house in Munich was too small for these great spectacles. Wagner suggested that a theater be built from his own designs. The king approved the project, and the outcome was the famous Wagnerian Festival Theater in Bayreuth, Bavaria. The first Wagnerian festival was held in this theater in 1876.

Wagner's first wife had died in 1866, and in 1870 he

A scene from Richard Wagner's opera *Parsifal*.
Michael Latz/AFP/Getty Images

married Cosima von Bülow, the daughter of Franz Liszt. She had been the wife of Wagner's close friend and colleague, Hans von Bülow, but she deserted him for Wagner. In 1879 Wagner's health began to fail, and he spent the winters in Venice. There he died in 1883, and his body was taken to Bayreuth for burial.

Wagner's music dramas, especially those based on the Nibelung tales, are his most notable works. These include *Das Rheingold* (*The Rhine Gold*), *Die Walküre* (*The Valkyrie*), *Siegfried*, and *Götterdämmerung* (*The Twilight of the Gods*). *Tristan und Isolde* (*Tristan and Isolde*) and *Parsifal* are part of the King Arthur cycle. *Die Meistersinger von Nürnberg* (*The Mastersingers of Nuremberg*) is the story of the cobbler Hans Sachs.

KANYE WEST

(b. 1977–)

U.S. producer and rapper West turned his production success in the late 1990s and early 2000s into a career as a popular, critically acclaimed solo artist. As a producer he developed his own distinctive style, sampling classic hit songs and inventively incorporating them into rap songs. As a performer West distinguished himself by fusing commercially appealing rap with politically aware themes and lyrics.

Kanye West was born on June 8, 1977, in Atlanta, Ga. He grew up in Chicago, Ill., and attended Chicago State University for one year before dropping out to pursue a career in music. Early on he demonstrated his considerable abilities as a producer, working with such artists as Jermaine Dupri and Mase. After relocating to the New York City area, he made his name with his production work for Roc-a-Fella Records, especially on rapper Jay-Z's album *The Blueprint* (2001).

Although criticized by some major record labels for not possessing the tough "street" image that most hip-hop artists cultivated, West continued to compose and record his own songs, eventually releasing his debut solo album, *The College Dropout*, in 2004. It was critically and commercially successful. West used clever wordplay to blend humor, faith, insight, and political awareness on songs such as "Through the Wire" and the gospel-choir-backed "Jesus Walks." He won several Grammy Awards for his work on the album, and he quickly rose to stardom. His second album, *Late Registration* (2005), repeated the commercial success of his first, with a number of hit singles, including "Diamonds in Sierra Leone" and "Gold Digger." The album earned West three more Grammy Awards.

Throughout his career, West continued to produce for high-profile artists such as Ludacris, Alicia Keys, and Janet Jackson. He also founded GOOD Music, a record label under the auspices of Sony BMG. His third release, *Graduation* (2007), produced the hit singles "Good Life" and "Stronger" and garnered him four more Grammy Awards. In 2008 West released *808s and Heartbreak*, an album that dwelled on feelings of personal loss and regret. Its sound differed radically from his previous releases, as West chose to sing (with the assistance of the vocal production tool Auto-Tune) rather than rap many of his lyrics.

West spent much of late 2009 rehabilitating his image. He had rushed the stage at the MTV Video Music Awards, preempting Taylor Swift's acceptance speech for best female video, to declare that, "Beyoncé had one of the best videos of all time." Video footage of the incident quickly went viral on the Internet, and West found himself scolded by the media. A series of apologies, some of them appearing as a stream-of-consciousness narrative on West's Twitter feed, soon followed.

The brashness that caused him such trouble in 2009 fueled a triumphant return to music the following year with *My Beautiful Dark Twisted Fantasy*, a monumentally complex exploration of the nature of success and celebrity. With potent rhymes, instrumentation that ranged from tribal drums to soaring orchestral accompaniment, and a list of guest performers that included Jay-Z, Rihanna, Kid Cudi, and Chris Rock, the album represented some of West's most ambitious work, and it was rewarded with a trio of Grammy Awards. He followed it with *Watch the Throne* (2011), a Billboard chart-topping collaboration with Jay-Z that featured the Grammy-winning singles "Otis" and "N****s in Paris." In 2012 West presented *Cruel Summer*, a compilation album featuring him and some of the artists signed to his GOOD Music label.

In 2013, West released his sixth album *Yeezus* (a portmanteau of the rapper's nickname "Yeezy" and the name of Jesus), employing guerilla marketing techniques in promotion of the album, including public video projectors, cryptic Twitter messages, and his own website to announce details of its release. Its commercialization of underground genres such as Chicago drill and acid house garnered high critical acclaim, and the album sold well on its release.

WHITE STRIPES

The White Stripes were an American rock duo from Detroit, Mich. known for combining punk, folk, country, and Mississippi Delta blues. The original band members were Jack White (b. John Anthony

Gillis; July 9, 1975, Detroit) and Meg White (b. Megan Martha White; Dec. 10, 1974, Grosse Pointe Farms, Mich.).

There was much speculation about whether guitarist-vocalist Jack White and drummer Meg White were brother and sister, as they often claimed, or husband and wife. Despite the eventual discovery by the media of a marriage license (1996) and a divorce certificate (2000), the pair remained enigmatic about the precise nature of their relationship.

During the 1990s Meg held a variety of service jobs, and Jack worked as a furniture upholsterer. Exposed to a wide range of music by his employer, Brian Muldoon, Jack became interested in the sound of Detroit punk pioneers Iggy and the Stooges and the MC5. Jack (on guitar) and Muldoon recorded a blues-infused single under the name the Upholsterers.

Trading one set of influences for another, in 1993 Jack signed on as drummer for the established "cow-punk" band Goober and the Peas. Jack gained experience onstage and in the recording studio, and the group's sound—a fusion of punk and rockabilly—and its stage persona (featuring cowboy hats and embroidered western suits) would reappear in his later work. In 1996 Goober and the Peas broke up, and Jack and Meg were married. That year the couple moved into Jack's childhood home, and they began to craft the sound of the White Stripes. The duo played at venues around Detroit, frequently appearing with Two-Star Tabernacle, a country-rock outfit that featured Jack and former Goober and the Peas front man Dan Miller. The White Stripes signed a contract with the independent Sympathy for the Record Industry label, and the duo's self-titled debut album was released in 1999. It was followed the next year by *De Stijl*.

In 2001 the White Stripes released their breakthrough album, *White Blood Cells*. Michel Gondry's eye-catching video for the single "Fell in Love with a Girl" received regular airplay on MTV, and the group became media darlings. The duo followed with *Elephant* (2003), a percussion-driven collection of songs that featured Meg's debut as a vocalist. *Elephant* earned a Grammy Award for best alternative music album, and it sold over a million copies on the strength of singles such as "Seven Nation Army." Jack appeared in the film *Cold Mountain* (2003), and he contributed five songs to its Grammy-nominated sound track.

He also produced country legend Loretta Lynn's *Van Lear Rose* (2004), a collection of honky-tonk anthems that earned a pair of Grammy Awards and introduced Lynn to a new generation of fans. The White Stripes earned another Grammy for their album *Get Behind Me Satan* (2005), and the song "Icky Thump," from their album of the same name (2007), became the band's first top 40 hit on the Billboard singles chart.

The White Stripes went on hiatus in 2007 after Meg was afflicted with performance-related anxiety. They returned to the stage for a single performance in February 2009 for the final episode of *Late Night with Conan O'Brien*. Continuing to expand his body of work, Jack experimented with straightforward power pop as a member of the Raconteurs. The quartet produced a pair of well-received albums (2006 and 2008) and quickly became a fixture on the summer concert circuit. Meg married guitarist Jackson Smith (son of rock legend Patti Smith) in May 2009, and Jack undertook yet another side project. Enlisting members of the Kills and Queens of the Stone Age, Jack formed the Dead Weather, a bluesy psychedelic rock combo whose debut album, *Horehound*, was released in July 2009.

In March 2009 Jack founded Third Man Records, a Nashville record store, performance space, and label. As the rest of the music industry was trying to adjust its business model to accommodate digital downloads, White's label embraced the physical artifacts of the album era: the turntable, the gatefold cover, and, above all, high-quality vinyl releases. As Jack spent more time on Third Man and other projects—he produced *The Party Ain't Over*, the 2011 comeback album from rockabilly legend Wanda Jackson—White Stripes fans began to suspect that the band's hiatus might be permanent. This was confirmed when in February 2011 Meg and Jack announced that they would no longer record or appear as the White Stripes. The following year Jack embarked on a solo career with the stylistically expansive Blunderbuss.

THE WHO

B ritish rock group the Who were among the most popular and influential bands of the 1960s and '70s. Though primarily inspired by

American rhythm and blues, the Who took a bold step toward defining a uniquely British rock sound in the 1960s. Shunning the Beatles' idealized romance and the Rolling Stones' cocky swagger, the Who straightforwardly dealt with teenage travails.

Pete Townshend (b. May 19, 1945) and John Entwistle (b. Oct. 9, 1944–d. June 27, 2002) joined Roger Daltrey (b. March 1, 1944) in his group, the Detours, in 1962; with drummer Doug Sandom they became, in turn, the Who and the High Numbers. Keith Moon (b. Aug. 23, 1946–d. Sept. 7, 1978) replaced Sandom in early 1964, after which the group released a self-consciously mod single ("I'm the Face") to little notice and became the Who again later that year. The West London quartet cultivated a Pop art image to suit the fashion-obsessed British mod subculture and matched that look with the rhythm-and-blues sound that mod youth favored. Townshend ultimately acknowledged that clothing made from the Union Jack (the British flag), sharp suits, pointy boots, and short haircuts were a contrivance, but it did the trick, locking in a fanatically devoted core following.

The band's early records dealt with alienation, uncertainty, and frustration, lashing out with tough lyrics, savage power chords and squalling feedback by guitarist-songwriter Townshend, the energizing assault of drummer Moon and bassist Entwistle, and the macho brawn of singer Daltrey. Four singles introduced the Who in 1965–66—"I Can't Explain," "Anyway, Anyhow, Anywhere," "My Generation," and "Substitute"— along with Townshend's habit of smashing his guitar to end concerts. While other groups were moving toward peace-and-love idealism, the Who sang of unrequited lust ("Pictures of Lily"), peer pressure ("Happy Jack"), creepy insects (Entwistle's "Boris the Spider"), and gender confusion ("I'm a Boy").

Until the 1967 release of *The Who Sell Out*, a sardonic concept album presented as a pirate radio broadcast, the Who were primarily a singles group. They were, however, more successful in this regard in Britain (eight top ten hits between 1965 and 1967) than in the United States ("I Can See for Miles," released in 1967, was the group's only Billboard top ten single). It was the 1969 rock opera *Tommy*—and a memorable performance at Woodstock that summer—that made the Who a world-class album-rock act.

The Who cemented their standing with *Who's Next* (1971), an album of would-be teen anthems ("Won't Get Fooled Again" and "Baba O'Riley") and sensitive romances ("Behind Blue Eyes" and "Love Ain't for Keeping"). That same year, Entwistle released a solo album, the darkly amusing *Smash Your Head Against the Wall*; Townshend issued his first solo album, *Who Came First*, in 1972; and Daltrey offered his, *Daltrey*, in 1973. Still, the Who continued apace, releasing Townshend's second magnum rock opera, *Quadrophenia*, in 1973, *The Who by Numbers* in 1975, and *Who Are You* in 1978.

Moon died of an accidental drug overdose in 1978 and was replaced by Kenney Jones (b. Sept. 16, 1948), who was formerly with the Small Faces and the Faces. The Who then released *Face Dances* (1981) and *It's Hard* (1982) before disbanding in 1982. Daltrey pursued acting while letting his solo career taper off. Entwistle released occasional records to little effect. Townshend busied himself briefly as a book editor while undertaking a variety of solo ventures, from fine Who-like rock records such as *Empty Glass* (1980) to the less-successful *The Iron Man* (1989), which reflected a growing interest in musical theater that culminated in his triumphant delivery of *Tommy* to Broadway in 1993. Townshend, Daltrey, and Entwistle reunited for tours in 1989 and 1996–97. The Who were about to embark on a U.S. tour in 2002 when Entwistle passed away.

HANK WILLIAMS

(b. 1923–d. 1953)

The American musician Hank Williams was one of the leading figures in country and western music who was also successful in the popular music market. His short turbulent life and his mournful tunes brought him an almost mythic status, and his recordings remain popular decades after his death.

Hiram King Williams was born in Georgiana, Ala., on Sept. 17, 1923. He taught himself to play the guitar at the age of eight, was writing songs at 12, and made his radio debut at 13. In 1937 he won an amateur contest for his own composition, "WPA Blues." That year, at age 14, he formed his first band, Hank Williams and his Drifting Cowboys. Exempted from military service because he suffered from spina bifida, Williams scraped by during the World War II years, playing in honky-tonks when possible, and for a period he worked as a welder in a shipyard. He married in 1944 and soon thereafter rekindled his music career.

Williams arrived in Nashville in 1946. His series of recordings in 1947 on the MGM label ("Move It on Over" was his first hit) won him national, and subsequently international, fame. In 1948 he moved to Shreveport, La., to perform on *Louisiana Hayride*, a popular weekly radio program. Williams's "Lovesick Blues" recording in 1949 was a smash hit, and he joined the Grand Ole Opry in Nashville that year. Among his best-selling recordings that followed were "Cold, Cold Heart," "Your Cheatin' Heart," "Long Gone Lonesome Blues," "I'm So Lonesome I Could Cry," and "Hey, Good Lookin'." Many of his songs found greater success after they were recorded by more-mainstream artists, such as "Cold, Cold Heart," which became a hit for Tony Bennett in 1951.

Appearing on network television programs and touring nationally, Williams began to gain appreciation by a wider audience, and he was soon pressed with songwriting requests and offers of a film career. However, long-term alcohol abuse, unsuccessful surgery for his spinal condition, and the dissolution of his marriage took its toll. By August 1952 he was dismissed from the Grand Ole Opry. His death of an apparent heart attack, on Jan. 1, 1953, in a car on the road to Oak Hill, W. Va., may have been the result of drug and alcohol abuse. His son, Hank Williams, Jr., sang his songs in a film biography, *Your Cheatin' Heart* (1964).

STEVIE WONDER

(b. 1950–)

U.S. singer, songwriter, producer, and musician Stevie Wonder, although blind since infancy, never lacked musical vision. Wonder's combination of soul, pop, funk, and rock earned him critical acclaim, including more than 20 Grammys and an Academy Award, and commercial success. With millions of records sold, the multitalented performer was recognized for his musical achievements as well as his social activism.

Born Steveland Judkins Morris on May 13, 1950, in Saginaw, Mich., Stevie was blinded shortly after his premature birth by a surfeit of oxygen in his incubator. In 1954 his family moved to Detroit, where he spent most of his youth and was exposed to gospel music in his Baptist church. He developed his musical talent early; by age 11 he had demonstrated a talent for singing and mastered piano, harmonica, and drums.

A friend introduced Stevie to Motown's Berry Gordy, who recognized the

Stevie Wonder. *Larry Busacca/Getty Images*

youngster's exceptional talent and took him under the label's wings. Barely a teenager, he was signed to Motown Records in 1963 and given the stage name Little Stevie Wonder. Success came quickly, as Wonder's third single, "Fingertips, Part 2," hit number one in the United States on both the pop and rhythm and blues charts in 1963. By the time he was 18, Wonder had released enough hits—such as "Uptight," "Nothing's Too Good for My Baby," "I Was Made to Love Her," and "For Once in My Life"—to fill his first *Greatest Hits* album in 1968. He followed that up with more hits, including the platinum-selling "My Cherie Amour" (1969) and "Signed, Sealed, Delivered, I'm Yours" (1970).

In 1970 Wonder married Syreeta Wright, a Motown employee and aspiring singer. The couple collaborated on several songs, and Wonder produced a few records for her. After two years of marriage, they divorced.

In 1971, at age 21, Wonder took some of his Motown earnings and started Black Bull Music, a music publishing company that would give him more creative freedom than he had with Motown. He used two albums that he recorded independently as leverage in negotiations with Motown, which subsequently offered him a more open contract that gave him complete artistic control over his music. He had begun experimenting with new musical forms, particularly through his innovative use of the synthesizer, when a serious automobile accident in 1973 almost claimed his life. Despite the personal difficulties it posed, this period yielded some of Wonder's most notable albums: *Talking Book* (1972), which included "You Are the Sunshine of My Life" and "Superstition"; *Innervisions* (1973), which included "Higher Ground"; *Fulfillingness' First Finale* (1974), which included "Boogie on Reggae Woman"; and *Songs in the Key of Life* (1976).

During the 1980s Wonder released fewer solo albums but made successful recordings with other artists. He collaborated with Paul McCartney on the antiracism hit single "Ebony and Ivory" (1982), with Chaka Khan on "I Feel for You" (1984), and with Dionne Warwick on "That's What Friends Are For" (1986), which he also performed for an AIDS benefit album. His single "I Just Called to Say I Love You," from the sound track of the film *The Woman in Red* won an Academy Award in 1985.

In 1989 Wonder was inducted into the Rock and Roll Hall of Fame. He signed a unique lifetime contract with Motown Records in 1992. *Conversation Peace*, an album Wonder labored over for nearly eight years before its 1995 release, drew positive reviews. Shortly thereafter he had a hit with *Natural Wonder* (1995), a live double CD supported with a concert tour.

In addition to his sizable music contributions, Wonder's career was distinguished by his political and social activism. Among other humanitarian causes, he lobbied for gun control, against drunk driving and South Africa's apartheid system, and on behalf of anti-hunger campaigns.

GLOSSARY

ACCORDION A musical instrument that has a keyboard and a bellows and that produces tones when air is forced past metal reeds.

ALEATORIC Characterized by chance or indeterminate elements.

AVANT-GARDE Describes new or experimental concepts especially in the arts.

BOSSA NOVA Popular music of Brazilian origin that is rhythmically related to the samba but with complex harmonies and improvised jazzlike passages.

CHANSON Music-hall or cabaret song.

CONTRALTO The lowest female signing voice, or a singer with such a voice.

CZAR The title for a ruler of Russia until the 1917 revolution.

DISENFRANCHISED Deprived of a legal right, particularly the right to vote.

EBULLIENT Having or showing liveliness and enthusiasm.

ECLECTIC Describes something made from various doctrines, methods, or styles.

ÉTUDE A piece of music for the practice of a point of technique

FALSETTO An artificially high voice.

FUNK Music that combines forms of blues, gospel, or soul music and has a strong backbeat.

HALLMARK A mark or indication of excellence, quality, or purity.

MAZURKA Piece of music for a type of fast Polish folk dance also known as the mazurka.

MEMOIR A story of a personal experience.

MNEMONIC Assisting or intended to assist memory.

NEUME Any of various symbols used in the notation of Gregorian chant.

ORATORIO Vocal and orchestral work usually dramatizing a religious subject without action or scenery.

POLONAISE A dignified 19th-century Polish dance.

POSTHUMOUSLY Following or occurring after one's death.

PRELUDE Short musical introduction or musical piece played at the beginning of a church services.

PSYCHEDELIC Of, relating to, or being a drug that produces abnormal often extreme mental effects, or imitating the effects of psychedelic drugs.

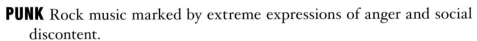

PUNK Rock music marked by extreme expressions of anger and social discontent.

QUINTET A musical composition for five instruments or voices.

REGGAE Popular music of Jamaican origin that combines native styles with elements of U.S. black popular music and is performed at moderate tempos with the accent on the offbeat.

SEXTET A musical composition for six instruments or voices.

SOLMIZATION The act, practice, or system of using syllables to denote the tones of a musical scale.

SYNCOPATED Describes a piece of music having the regular metrical accent temporarily displaced, typically caused by stressing the weak beat.

ZYDECO Popular music of southern Louisiana that combines tunes of French origin with elements of Caribbean music and the blues.

EMP Museum
325 5th Avenue N
Seattle, WA 98109
(206) 770-2700
Website: http://www.empmuseum.org
The EMP Museum hosts a wide variety of exhibits designed to engage visitors with the ideas and movements that fuel popular music and culture. Numerous events, workshops, performances, and more complement the Museum's mission of educating the public about the history of and current trends in music, film, and other cultural phenomena.

Jazz Museum in Harlem
104 East 126th Street, Suite 2D
New York, NY 10035
(212) 348-8300
Website: http://www.jazzmuseuminharlem.org
An affiliate of the Smithsonian Institution, the Jazz Museum in Harlem hosts a variety of programs dedicated to keeping the spirit of jazz alive in the neighborhood where it soared in the 1920s. Their Harlem Speaks series honors important figures in the jazz community, and their Jazz for Curious Listeners and Jazz for Curious Readers courses teach the public about the history and styles of jazz.

Memphis Rock 'n' Soul Museum
191 Beale Street, Suite 100
Memphis, TN 38103
(901) 205-2533
Website: http://memphisrocknsoul.org
The Memphis Rock 'n' Soul Museum features an exhibition about the birth of rock and soul music curated by the Smithsonian Institution. In addition to its educational exhibits on the influence of American music on global culture, it provides resources to educators for promoting American music history in school. In August 2004,

the museum became one of Memphis's most prominent features when it moved to a location on sight of the massive FedExForum sports arena.

Music Canada
85 Mowat Avenue
Toronto, ON M6K 3E3 Canada
(416) 967-7272
Website: http://www.musiccanada.com
Music Canada is a nonprofit trade organization founded in 1964 that works closely with recording studios, live music venues, concert promoters, and managers in the promotion and development of the music cluster in Canada. They work closely with the biggest record labels to advocate for and promote Canadian musicians' best interests.

Musician Rights Organization Canada
1200 Eglinton Avenue East, Suite 505
Toronto, ON M3C 1H9 Canada
(416) 510-0279
Website: http://musiciansrights.ca
The MROC is a non profit collective that collects and distributes royalties for Canadian performers. MROC provides music fans with important information and key links to relevant organizations, as well as educating on musicians' rights to their own music.

Rock and Roll Hall of Fame and Museum
1100 Rock and Roll Boulevard
Cleveland, OH 44114
(216) 781-7625
Website: http://www.rockhall.com
The Rock and Roll Hall of Fame and Museum is a nonprofit organization that educates visitors, fans, and scholars from around the world about the history and continuing significance of rock and roll. It carries out this mission through its operation of a world-class museum

that collects, preserves, exhibits, and interprets this art form and through its library and archives, as well as its educational programs.

WEBSITES

Due to the changing nature of Internet links, Rosen Publishing has developed an online list of Web sites related to the subject of this book. This site is updated regularly. Please use this link to access the list:

http://www.rosenlinks.com/pysk/music

FOR FURTHER READING

Anderson, Jennifer Joline. *How to Analyze the Music of Michael Jackson*. Edina, MN: ABDO, 2011.

Aretha, David. *Awesome African-American Rock and Soul Musicians*. Berkeley Heights, NJ: Enslow, 2012.

Carew-Miller, Anna. *Ludwig van Beethoven: Great Composer*. Broomall, PA: Mason Crest, 2013.

Cook, Diane. *Wolfgang Amadeus Mozart: World-Famous Composer*. Broomall, PA: Mason Crest, 2013.

Feinstein, Stephen. *Incredible African-American Jazz Musicians*. Berkeley Heights, NJ: Enslow, 2012.

Kallen, Stuart A. *The History of American Pop*. San Diego, CA: Lucent Books, 2012.

Kallen, Stuart A. *The History of Rock and Roll*. San Diego, CA: Lucent Books, 2012.

Partridge, Kenneth. *Louis Armstrong: Musician*. New York: Chelsea House, 2011.

Ray, Michael. *Alternative, Country, Hip-Hop, Rap, and More: Music from the 1980s to Today*. New York, NY: Rosen Publishing, 2012.

Ray, Michael. *Disco, Punk, New Wave, Heavy Metal, and More: Music in the 1970s and 1980s*. New York, NY: Rosen Publishing, 2012.

INDEX

A

A&M Records, 127
Adele, 1–2
Adler, Eric "Vietnam," 113
Allman, Duane, 34
Anthrax, 113
Apollo Theater, 50, 136
Arista Records, 112
Armstrong, Louis, 3–4, 51, 66
Atlantic Records, 53

B

Bach, Carl Philipp Emanuel, 6
Bach, Johann Christian, 6, 99
Bach, Johann Sebastian, 4–6, 23, 95,
     130, 146
Bach, Wilhelm Friedemann, 6
Baez, Joan, 46
Baker, Ginger, 33, 34
Band, the, 45, 46
Barnett, Angela, 21
Baroque period, 6, 64
Bartók, Béla, 6–7, 59
Basie, Count, 7–8, 51, 52, 58, 66, 69
Beach Boys, the, 9–10
Beatles, the, 11–13, 46, 86, 88, 120, 129, 152
Bee Gees, the, 14–15
Beethoven, Ludwig van, 6, 15–18, 23, 64,
     87, 95, 130
Bellini, Vincenzo, 28, 108
Bennett, Tony, 154
Bernstein, Leonard, 18–19
Berry, Chuck, 9, 19, 67, 88, 100, 120
Best, Pete, 11
Beyoncé, 79, 149
Big Bopper, the, 70, 71
Black Sabbath, 20, 86
Blige, Mary J., 79

Blind Faith, 33, 34
Blue Grass Boys, 98
Bolan, Marc, 22
Bomb Squad, the, 113
Bonham, Jason, 86
Bonham, John, 85–86
Bono, 142
Bowie, David, 20–23
Brahms, Johannes, 23–24, 123
Bramlett, Delaney and Bonnie, 34
Brown, James, 24–26, 106
Browne, Jackson, 97
Bruce, Jack, 33
Buckley, Jeff, 117
Butler, Terry "Geezer," 20
Byrds, the, 45, 96

C

Cage, John, 26–27
Callas, Maria, 27–28
Campbell, Glen, 10
Capitol Records, 9, 134
Carreras, José, 43, 108
Chandler, Chas, 67
Charles, Ray, 28–30, 53
Chenier, Clifton, 30–31
Cher, 45
Chess Records, 19, 52, 102, 137
Chimes, Terry, 35
Chopin, Frédéric, 31–33, 41
Christian, Charlie, 81
Chuck D, 113
Clapton, Eric, 10, 33–35, 46, 100
Clash, the, 35–37
Clayton, Adam, 142
Cline, Patsy, 37–38
Clinton, Bill, 107
Clinton, George, 106, 107
Cobain, Kurt, 103–104

Cochran, Eddie, 127
Cole, Nat King, 29, 38–39
Collins, Bootsy, 26, 106
Coltrane, John, 39
Columbia Records, 131, 133, 134
Cook, Paul, 126, 127
Cooke, Sam, 67
Cotton Club, 47
Country Music Hall of Fame, 38, 98
Cream, 33, 34, 35
Crickets, the, 11, 70–71
Crosby, David, 96
Cruz, Celia, 116
Cunningham, Merce, 27
Czerny, Karl, 87

D

Daltrey, Roger, 152, 153
Davis, Miles, 39–40, 105
Davis, Sammy, Jr., 133, 134
Debussy, Claude, 40–41
Decca Records, 37, 38, 70
Def Jam Recordings, 78, 79, 113, 114
Denver, John, 42
Derek and the Dominos, 34
Diaghilev, Sergei, 140
Dixon, Willie, 102
Domingo, Plácido, 41–44, 108
Donizetti's, Gaetano, 28, 107
Dorsey, Tommy, 74, 133
Dr. Dre, 48, 49, 50
D12, 49
Dylan, Bob, 44–47, 68, 100, 136

E

Earth, Wind & Fire, 106
Edge, the, 142
Ellington, Duke, 8, 47–48, 51, 58, 69

Elliot, Ramblin' Jack, 46
EMI, 118, 126
Eminem, 48–50
Eno, Brian, 22
Entwistle, John, 152, 153
Epic Records, 75
Epstein, Brian, 11–12
E Street Band, 138, 139
Everly Brothers, 14

F

Faces, the, 153
Farrow, Mia, 134
50 Cent, 49, 50
Fitzgerald, Ella, 50–51
Flavor Flav, 113
Franklin, Aretha, 51–53

G

Gardner, Ava, 134
Garfunkel, Art, 130–132
Gaye, Marvin, 136, 137
Gershwin, George, 51, 53–55, 105
Gershwin, Ira, 50, 51, 53–55
Gibb, Barry, 14
Gibb, Maurice, 14
Gibb, Robin, 14
Gilbert, William Schwenck, 55–56, 109
Gillespie, Dizzy, 105
Ginsberg, Allen, 46, 57
Glass, Philip, 56–57, 129
Godrich, Nigel, 118
Goodman, Benny, 57–59, 66, 69, 133
Gordy, Berry, 136, 137, 155
Grammy Awards, 2, 29, 35, 46, 49, 50, 51,
    76, 78, 79, 90, 97, 99, 108, 116, 118,
    122, 131, 132, 134, 139, 144, 148, 149,
    150, 151, 154

Grand Ole Opry, 37, 38, 98, 154
Grateful Dead, 106
Grech, Rick, 34
Greenwood, Colin, 117
Greenwood, Jonny, 117, 118
Grohl, Dave, 103–104
grunge, 103
Guido d'Arezzo, 59–60
Guthrie, Arlo, 61
Guthrie, Woody, 61–62, 125
Guy, Buddy, 102

H

Handel, George Frideric, 62–63
Handy, W.C., 63–64, 65
Harrison, George, 11–13, 34, 46, 129
Haydn, Joseph, 6, 16, 17, 64–65, 99, 122
Hays, Lee, 125
Hazel, Eddie, 106
Headon, Nick, 35
heavy metal, 20, 85, 86, 104
Helm, Levon, 45
Henderson, Fletcher, 58, 65–67, 69
Hendrix, Jimi, 34, 67–69, 100, 129
Hole, 104
Holiday, Billie, 52, 69–70, 135
Holly, Buddy, 11, 70–71
House, Son, 80, 101
Howlin' Wolf, 85

I

Ice Cube, 107
Iggy and the Stooges, 126, 150
Iman, 23
Iommi, Tony, 20
Isley Brothers, 67
Ives, Charles, 71–73, 122

J

Jackson, Janet, 148
Jackson, Mahalia, 73–74, 135
Jackson, Michael, 75–77
Jackson, Wanda, 151
Jackson 5, 75, 77
Jagger, Mick, 120, 122
James, Etta, 1
Jardine, Michael, 9
Jay-Z, 77–79, 148, 149
Jimi Hendrix Experience, 67–68
Joachim, Joseph, 24
John, Elton, 10, 49
Johnson, Robert, 33, 79–80, 101
Johnston, Bruce, 9, 10
Jones, Brian, 120, 121
Jones, John Paul, 85
Jones, Kenney, 153
Jones, Mick, 35, 36
Jones, Steve, 126, 127
Joplin, Janis, 135
Josquin des Prez, 80–81
Juilliard School, 39, 56, 115, 125

K

Kennedy Center Honors, 10, 30, 46, 108
Keys, Alicia, 79, 148
Khan, Chaka, 156
Kills, the, 151
King, B.B., 67, 81–82
King, Martin Luther, Jr., 74
Knopfler, Mark, 46
Kulthūm, Umm, 82–84

L

Lampell, Millard, 125
La Scala, 28, 42, 115, 145

Leadbelly, 84
Led Zeppelin, 85–86
Lennon, John, 11–13, 120
Lil Wayne, 79
Linkin Park, 79
Liszt, Franz, 86–87, 147
Little Richard, 21, 25, 67, 88–89
Lollapalooza, 107
Lomax, Alan, 102
Love, Courtney, 104
Love, Michael, 9
Ludacris, 148
Lynn, Loretta, 38, 151

M

Madonna, 89–91
Mahler, Gustav, 91–92
Mancini, Henry, 42
Marks, David, 9
Marley, Bob, 92–95
Marley, Rita, 94
Martin, Dean, 133
Martin, George, 12
Martini, Giovanni Battista, 99
Marx, Barbara, 134
Matlock, Glen, 126, 127
Mayall, John, 33
Mayfield, Curtis, 67
McCartney, Linda, 13
McCartney, Paul, 10, 11–13, 76, 120, 156
MC5, 150
McGuinn, Roger, 46
McLaren, Malcolm, 126, 127
Mendelssohn, Felix, 95–96
Metropolitan Opera, 42, 43, 44, 92, 107, 114
M.I.A., 90
Minaj, Nicki, 91
Mingus, Charles, 97

Minnelli, Liza, 134
Mitchell, Joni, 96–97
Mitchell, Mitch, 67
Monk, Thelonious, 105
Monkees, the, 21, 68
Monroe, Bill, 97–99
Moon, Keith, 152, 153
Moore, Warren, 136
Mothers of Invention, 33–34
Motown Records, 52, 75, 106, 136, 155, 156
Mott the Hoople, 22
Mozart, Wolfgang Amadeus, 6, 16, 17, 44, 59, 64, 99–101, 122
MTV, 20, 49, 76, 149, 150
Muddy Waters, 19, 33, 67, 85, 101–102, 120
Mullen, Larry, Jr., 142

N

Nash, Graham, 97
Nelson, Willie, 38
Neptunes, the, 90
New York Dolls, 126
New York Philharmonic, 18, 19, 92
Nirvana, 86, 103–104, 117
Nolan, Jimmy, 26
Novoselic, Krist, 103–104
N.W.A., 48, 114

O

O'Brien, Ed, 117
Ocean, Frank, 79
Ono, Yoko, 13
Orbison, Roy, 46
Osbourne, Ozzy, 20

P

Page, Jimmy, 85–86
Parker, Charlie, 39, 104–105

Parker, Colonel Tom, 110, 111
Parker, Maceo, 26
Parks, Rosa, 74
Parliament-Funkadelic, 106–107
Pavarotti, Luciano, 43, 107–108
Penn, Sean, 91
Peter, Paul, and Mary, 45
Petty, Norman, 70, 71
Petty, Tom, 46
Phillips, Julianne, 139
Phillips, Sam, 110
Piaf, Edith, 108–109
Pink Floyd, 117
Pixies, 117
Plant, Robert, 85–86
Pons, Lily, 42
Porter, Cole, 51, 109–110
Presley, Elvis, 21, 70, 77, 88, 110–111, 138
Presley, Lisa Marie, 77, 111
Presley, Priscilla, 111
Primettes, the, 136–137
Prince, 112
Professor Griff, 113
Public Enemy, 112–114
Puccini, Giacomo, 28, 107, 114–115
Puente, Tito, 115–116
punk rock, 35–37

Q

Queen, 23
Queens of the Stone Age, 151

R

Raconteurs, the, 151
Radiohead, 116–118
Rainey, Ma, 135
Raitt, Bonnie, 101
RCA Records/RCA Victor, 98, 110

Redding, Noel, 67
Redding, Otis, 53
Reed, Lou, 22
Reinhardt, Django, 81
R.E.M., 117
Reprise Records, 134
Richards, Keith, 120, 122
Richie, Lionel, 77
Riddle, Nelson, 134
Rihanna, 79, 149
Rimski-Korsakov, Nikolai, 140
Ritchie, Guy, 91
Robertson, Robbie, 45
Robinson, Smokey, 136–137
Roc-a-Fella Records, 78, 148
Rock and Roll Hall of Fame, 10, 15, 19, 20, 23, 26, 30, 35, 46, 51, 69, 71, 74, 77, 80, 86, 89, 97, 98, 102, 107, 114, 122, 126, 127, 132, 137, 144, 156
Rodgers, Jimmie, 119–120
Rogers, Bobby, 136
Rogers, Claudette, 136, 137
Rogers, Kenny, 15
Rolling Stones, the, 86, 101, 120–122, 152
Romantic movement, 15, 32, 64
Ross, Diana, 15, 76, 136
Rotten, Johnny, 126, 127
Rubin, Rick, 2, 113

S

Salieri, Antonio, 16, 87, 124
Sandom, Doug, 152
Saturday Night Fever, 14, 15
Schoenberg, Arnold, 72, 122–123
Schubert, Franz, 123–124
Schumann, Clara, 24
Schumann, Robert, 24
Scialfa, Patti, 139
Scorsese, Martin, 46

Scriabin, Aleksander, 130
Seeger, Pete, 61, 124–126
Selway, Phil, 117
Sex Pistols, the, 35, 37, 126–127
Shankar, Ravi, 128–129
Shocklee, Hank, 113
Shocklee, Keith, 113
Shostakovich, Dmitri, 130
Simon, Paul, 130–132
Simon and Garfunkel, 130–132
Simonon, Paul, 35, 36
Sinatra, Frank, 132–135
Small Faces, the, 126, 153
Smith, Bessie, 73, 135
Smith, Jackson, 151
Smith, Patti, 151
Smokey Robinson and the Miracles, 136–137
Snoop Doggy Dogg, 114
Springsteen, Bruce, 137–139
Spungen, Nancy, 127
Starr, Ringo, 11–13
Stephney, Bill, 113
Stigwood, Robert, 14–15
Strauss, Richard, 6
Stravinsky, Igor, 72, 139–141
Streisand, Barbra, 15
Strummer, Joe, 35, 36
Sullivan, Arthur, 55–56, 109
Sun Records, 110
Supremes, the, 137
Sutcliffe, Stu, 11
Sutherland, Joan, 42
Swift, Taylor, 149

T

Tarplin, Marv, 136
Taylor, James, 97
Taylor, Mick, 46, 121

Tchaikovsky, Peter Ilich, 130, 141–142
Temptations, the, 136
Terminator X, 113
The-Dream, 79
Three Tenors, 43, 108
T.I., 79
Timbaland, 79, 90
Timberlake, Justin, 90
Tosh, Peter, 93
Townshend, Pete, 152, 153
Turner, Ike, 67
Turner, Tina, 67
Turtles, the, 45

U

U2, 142–144

V

Valens, Richie, 70, 71
Vandross, Luther, 53
Vaughan, Sarah, 136
Vaughn, Stevie Ray, 35
Verdi, Giuseppe, 28, 42, 44, 107, 114, 144–145
Vicious, Sid, 126, 127
Vienna Choir Boys, 124
Virgin Records, 127
Vivaldi, Antonio, 5, 145–146
von Meck, Nadezhda, 141, 142

W

Wagner, Richard, 44, 87, 123, 146–147
Wailer, Bunny, 93
Wailers, the, 92, 93, 94
Walker, T-Bone, 81
Walter, Bruno, 91
Ward, Bill, 20

Warhol, Andy, 23, 122
Warner Brothers/Warner Bros., 10, 112
Warwick, Dionne, 15, 156
Watts, Charlie, 120
Webber, Andrew Lloyd, 42
Weber, Constanze, 100
Wells, Mary, 136, 137
Wesley, Fred, 26
West, Kanye, 79, 148–149
White, Jack, 149–151
White, Meg, 150, 151
White, Ronnie, 136
White Stripes, 149–151
Who, the, 126, 129, 151–153
Williams, Hank, 153–154
Williams, Hank, Jr., 154
Williams, Pharrell, 90
Williamson, Sonny Boy, 33
Wilson, Brian, 9–10
Wilson, Carl, 9
Wilson, Carnie, 10
Wilson, Dennis, 9

Wilson, Jackie, 136
Wilson, Wendy, 10
Winehouse, Amy, 2
Wings, 13
Winwood, Steve, 34
Wonder, Stevie, 154–156
Wood, Ron, 121
Woodstock, 68, 152
Worrell, Bernie, 106
Wright, Syreeta, 155
Wyman, Bill, 120

Y

Yardbirds, the, 33, 35, 85
Yo-Yo, 107
Yorke, Thom, 117–118

Z

Zappa, Frank, 33–34
zydeco, 30–31